MW01132310

The Guide to
Winning a
Teaching Position

In ANY Job Market ™

GET THE EDGE – **THE INSIDE TRACK -** with this how-to guide! Learn about the job search, application, and hiring process. Learn to develop high quality application materials and improve your interview skills – *before you submit your job applications and your first interview.*

In this guide, read about <u>five winning strategies</u>, templates and examples of résumés, cover letters, and thank you letters. Read possible responses to more than 30 typical interview and questions – what to say and what not to say. And, receive practical advice from school personnel who hire experienced teachers and recent graduates.

To purchase additional books, visit http://www.winateachingjob.com.

MacGregor Kniseley, Ed.D.
Rhode Island College

About the Author

Professor Kniseley began his 35-year career in education as a teacher employed in non-school environmental education programs. Next, he taught for ten years in elementary and middle schools. Since 1990 he has been Professor of Elementary Education at Rhode Island College. He conducts a practical, interactive workshop-style course called CURR 480 *Winning a Teaching Position in Any Job Market*. Students learn about the job search and hiring process, how to develop cover letters, résumés, and hiring portfolios and how to improve their interview skills. And, students engage in mock job interviews with PreK-12 school personnel and college faculty who provide feedback. Contact him at HM 209, Department of Elementary Education, Rhode Island College, 600 Mt. Pleasant Ave., Providence RI 02908 p - 401-456-8865 e - mkniseley2@gmail.com, website: http://www.winateachingjob.com

Table of Contents

Acknowledgements

Experience is the best teacher. This book is based on a 35-year career as a teacher and professor of field-based education courses at Rhode Island College.

My sincere thanks for the support and expertise of the following people:

Roger Eldridge supported the development of the Rhode Island College course, CURR 480 Winning a Teaching Position in Any Job Market course and research on important selection factors.

Director of Rhode Island College Career Development Center, Linda Kent Davis, and her staff, Demetria Moran and Kathryn Sasso taught me about career development, searching and applying for jobs, interviewing, and ways to help people achieve their career goals.

Many volunteer Rhode Island PreK-12 educators and Rhode Island College faculty have served as interviewers for the "mock job interviews." Rhode Island College professors who contributed responses to typical interview questions include Nancy Cloud, Roger Eldridge, Rudolf Kraus, Paul LaCava, Corinne McKamey, Lisa Owen, and Robert Rude.

Gail Hareld (Providence RI Public Schools Human Resources), Shannon Sweeney Saunders (Warwick RI Public School Human Resources Department), Daniel Smith (Coventry RI Public Schools), and Patricia Whalen (East Providence RI Public Schools Human Resources Department) provided advice about the job search, application and hiring process.

Melissa Vesey and Rebecca Zakin, Rhode Island College MAT graduates, assisted me in interviewing principals about important selection factors in hiring job applicants.

William Oehlkers and Kathryn Sasso provided editorial assistance.

Scott Badger and Clark Baker provided valuable technical assistance.

And, my Rhode Island College students provided feedback and advice and helped to shape the content.

Introduction

This is my student teaching semester. I'm feeling increasingly confident about my abilities to teach. The feedback from my cooperating teacher and college supervisor has been really positive. Both say I have what it takes to be a professional teacher. I can't wait to graduate and realize my lifelong dream of teaching. But, my college supervisor presented the annual report of educator supply and demand. She explained that our graduating class is entering a job market with a surplus of teachers. The population is stagnant. The districts are reducing their budgets due to the deep recession. Recently hired teachers received "pink slips." There are no promises of open positions due to retirements. The competition is fierce. These are extraordinary times.

I wonder, Will I get a job and realize my dream?

Extraordinary times require extraordinary measures.

You're reading the Guide to Winning a Teaching Position because you're preparing to graduate, recently graduated, or you're an experienced teacher searching for a new job. Although focused on current education students, the strategies outlined within apply to all education job seekers. You want expert advice about winning the perfect teaching position ***before you submit your job applications and go for your first interview.***

Clearly, economic conditions are affecting the demand for teachers. In some areas where the population is declining, districts are closing schools, increasing class sizes and paring their rosters. We know from educator supply and demand research (AAEE, Bureau of Labor/Statistics) that tight job markets exist in the Great Lakes and Northeast regions. Generally, job prospects are better in urban and rural areas than in suburban districts. There's a surplus of elementary classroom, social studies, health and physical education teachers but a higher demand for special education, physics, chemistry, mathematics, bilingual education, and foreign language teachers.

We also know that numerous applicants are unable to win a teaching position because they are reluctant to search beyond the 50-mile radius of their home, university or college. Linda Kent Davis, director of Rhode Island College's Career Development Center, asks students this question to help them consider their future: "Is my career goal to teach? Or is it to teach in Rhode Island? Because those are very different questions." If you can't leave your home, you'll need to work harder to get your foot inside the door. Keep your doors open!

Most teachers don't.get hired after their first interview. They underestimate the time and effort it takes to prepare for the job search, applications and hiring process. Winning a teaching position in any job market requires tremendous effort, persistence, marketing and strategic thinking. You need to get organized and develop a plan of action. Get the edge and inside track on the hiring process *before your first interview!* Improve your chances of winning a job by learning about the job search and application process, researching schools, developing effective application materials, the art of interviewing, and posting online applications.

There are no secrets to winning the perfect teaching job. It is the result of preparation, persistence, hard work, and learning from experience. I've outlined FIVE WINNING STRATEGIES and included seven tactics associated with them that will improve your job search and maximize your chances for success. While there is no guarantee that using this Guide will result in a teaching position, it can significantly increase your chances.

Best of luck,

MacGregor Kniseley, Ed.D.
Rhode Island College

Five Winning Strategies

1. **Get organized and learn about the hiring process.** If you're a current teacher education student or recent graduate, meet with a career counselor at your college or university as soon as possible. Learn about the hiring process, educator supply and demand of teaching jobs by field and region, and how much teachers are paid. You will be submitting dozens of applications, so keep track of your applications. Create a centralized location (e.g., SchoolSpring.com or Interfolio.com) for storing and managing credentials and other job search documents. Enroll in career center workshops to fine-tune job application materials, interview skills, and design a professional image. Clean up your social networking sites and develop a professional email address. See ORGANIZE AND NETWORK.

2. **Know your school or district employer.** Consider the selection factors used by employers to hire teachers. Before applying for a specific teaching position, research the school or district hiring processes and criteria for hiring. Read job descriptions carefully and learn about the school's mission, initiatives, curriculum, and standards. See RESEARCH SCHOOLS.

3. **Increase your opportunities.** Conduct a search for positions in regions of the country with greater demand. Search for positions at central job posting sites for public and nonpublic schools and career fairs. Earn endorsements beyond initial certification in high demand fields. Monitor job posting sites beginning in January and through the spring and summer. See POST ONLINE APPLICATIONS.

4. **Promote yourself and network.** Applying for a job has been described as "shameless self-promotion." Learn to market yourself. Develop a compelling, customized cover letter, résumé, and hiring portfolio. Carefully format and proofread your job applications. Identify and contact 3-5 references. Send your references thank you letters after they write a letter of recommendation. Also, inform your professors, teachers, and principals that you are seeking a job. See COMPOSE A RÉSUMÉ AND COVER LETTER, DEVELOP A HIRING PORTFOLIO, and CONTACT REFERENCES.

5. **Know the selection criteria used by interviewers who make judgments about applicants. Practice interviewing.** Understand what character traits (e.g., critical reflection, personal responsibility, and constant learning) and leadership skills employers are seeking. Practice responding to typical interview questions with experienced teachers and professors and get their feedback. Communicate your knowledge of teaching and dispositions toward students. Relate to school's mission, initiatives, curriculum and standards. After the interview, send hand-written thank you cards to the interviewers. See PREPARE FOR INTERVIEWS.

Good luck with achieving success and winning the perfect teaching job!
If you have prepared well for this day, you deserve it!

Organize and Network

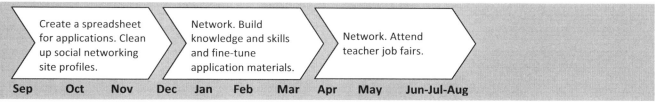

Create a spreadsheet for applications. Clean up social networking site profiles.

Network. Build knowledge and skills and fine-tune application materials.

Network. Attend teacher job fairs.

| Sep | Oct | Nov | Dec | Jan | Feb | Mar | Apr | May | Jun-Jul-Aug |

Visit a career counselor at a nearby college career center. Don't go through the process alone. Get support. Schedule an appointment with a career counselor to discuss the supply and demand for teachers in the region and across the country. Learn about college, regional, and district job fairs and services provided by the center to improve your résumé, cover letter, hiring portfolio, and interviewing skills.

Create a spreadsheet for job applications. If you're applying for teaching positions in a tight market, chances are you will submit dozens of applications. Create a file with folders of job descriptions and application materials. Maintain a chart with school district addresses, contact people, email, phone numbers, district web sites and job postings. Enter the dates that you submitted the application materials and followed up with thank you letters.

Clean up social networking web sites. Personal information on the web can support or hinder your chances of getting a job. Hiring committees use search engines to locate publicly available data on the Internet to learn about job applicants. Parents on the hiring committee are thinking about their child gaining access to any public sites. "Google" yourself. Review your social networking sites or web pages and check for public access. Clean up the websites and create a professional image. Remove inappropriate photographs and videos. Proofread the text.

Use a professional tone when emailing and speaking on the phone, or recording your voicemail message. In your voicemail message, identify yourself using both your first and last name and your phone number. Ask callers to leave their phone number and any specific requests they have.

Also, assure them you will return the call as soon as possible. Use a professional email username. *Sexybabe@hotmail.com* won't cut it. Good examples are MariaSantos@xxx.xxx, Maria.Santos@xxx.xxx, or msantos@xxx.xxx.

Network. List and contact people you know or who have observed you teach. During your teacher education program, you have many "networking" opportunities with teachers and principals. After you conduct an observation or complete a practical teaching experience, write a thank you letter to the teacher or principal. During student teaching, invite the principal to observe you teach. Following the observation, schedule a meeting with the principal. Prepare yourself well for this meeting. This is a chance to promote yourself further and practice interviewing.

Let them know you will be applying for teaching positions and ask them to let you know if there are any openings. Ask a principal, college supervisor, cooperating teacher and pre-student teaching clinical instructors to serve as references.

Build knowledge and skills and fine-tune application materials. Enroll in workshops and courses offered by your college career center on the job search, writing cover letters and résumés, and interviewing.

Attend teacher job fairs. Many colleges and larger school districts offer education career or teacher recruitment fairs in which hiring professionals from schools and school districts interview qualified job seekers. Participants register for four or five first round interviews during the day. American Association for Employment in Education lists education job fairs across the country.

Keeping Track

Following graduation, job applicants are submitting 10 to more than 50 job applications. So, it's likely that you will be submitting many applications. Create a table like the one below using a word-processing or spreadsheet application to keep track school or district job posting information, application due dates, tasks, and dates completed.

APPLICATION INFORMATION					TASKS AND DATE COMPLETED					
School District	Web Site	Job Posting	App Due	Who to Contact	Cover Letter	Ré-sumé	Es-say	Three References	Inter-view	Thank You Letter
Providence Public Schools	www.pps.org/	www.providenceschools.org/human resources	6/15	Ms. Maria Santos	4/7	4/7	4/7	1. Dr. P.-Yes 2. Ms S.-Yes 3. Mr. W.-Yes	5/15	
Warwick Public Schools	www.wps.org/	www.warwickschools.org/hremployment	6/30	Ms. Susan Smith	4/15	4/15	Not Req.	1. Dr. P.-Yes 2. Ms S.- 3. Mr. W.-		
Coventry Public Schools	www.cps.org	www.schoolspring.com/jobs	7/15	Mr. William Jones	4/30	4/30	Not Req.	1. Dr. P.-Yes 2. Ms S.- 3. Mr. W.-Yes		

Teacher Job Fairs

School districts and college career centers organize annual one-day teacher job fairs that bring together hiring personnel, other teacher recruiters, and job applicants. Most job fairs are face-to-face, but online teacher job fairs are increasing. Online fairs enable you to visit booths, browse for jobs, and interact real-time in chat rooms. And, they're open 24 hours a day.

You can find a monthly calendar of teacher job fairs across the country at American Association for Employment in Education web site. Larger districts will post district teacher job fairs at the human resources/employment web page.

Representatives from district human resources departments try to recruit job seekers and promote their districts. They receive résumés and pre-screen candidates in brief 10-15 minute individual or small group interviews. Often, job-seekers win future interviews with the district.

At teacher job fairs, job seekers learn about school districts, job openings and network. Sometimes there are workshops on composing high quality résumés and cover letters, applying to online teacher recruitment and hiring sites, and developing hiring portfolios.

Preparing for the Job Fair

You can prepare for a job fair by developing a one-page cover letter and a two-page résumé printed on high quality paper, a printed hiring portfolio, and CDs of e-portfolios. Place the cover letter on top of the résumé. Don't staple it. Instead, use a paper clip. Insert the CD in an individual CD envelope. Label the CD and indicate which file to open first. Make 10-15 copies.

Learn about the school district by visiting their web sites. Prepare and practice a 1-2 minute presentation about your career objective and qualifications that introduces you to the hiring personnel. Sometimes you can sign up in advance for interviews with districts when you enroll in the job fair.

Dress conservatively. Men should wear a dark or gray two-piece suit with a silk tie and polished shoes. Women should wear a dress or pant suit, collared blouse, and closed-toe shoes. Go easy on jewelry and cosmetics. Don't carry a backpack. Bring a small briefcase or business-like tote bag containing your hiring portfolio, a folder of résumés/cover letters, a notepad, pen, and a laptop. And, don't forget to turn off your cell phone before you enter the fair.

Checklist for a Teacher Job Fair

√	Items for Job Fair
	10 folders for cover letter, résumé, CD
	10 cover letters
	10 résumés
	10 CDs (e-Portfolio)
	Printed binder with hiring portfolio
	2 pens
	Notepad
	Small briefcase or business-tote bag
	Laptop (optional)
	Professional attire

Interviewing with Recruiters

When you meet with a recruiter at a teacher job fair, offer a firm handshake and introduce yourself. Open the folder with your résumé, cover letter and CD of your hiring portfolio. Then hand the folder to the recruiter. Make pleasant small talk and then deliver a brief 1-2 minute presentation about your career objective and qualifications. Listen to the recruiter talk about the district, benefits, and job opportunities. Ask questions and relate your knowledge, skills, and experiences to the job opportunity. Thank the recruiter for his/her time and express your interest in the position. Request a business card or ask for his/her name, title, and contact information.

Following the interview, take notes about each interview so you can refer to the conversation later in your thank you letter. After the job fair, email the recruiter a thank you letter. Use a business-style format. Write a sentence or two about something that came up in the conversation that relates to your knowledge, skills, and experience. Then, submit your application for the position. Mention in the cover letter that you met with the recruiter. Use the recruiter's name in the letter.

Research Schools

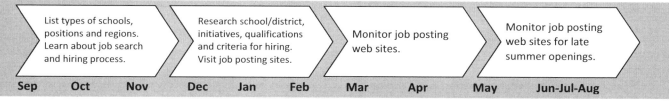

List types of schools, positions and regions. Learn about job search and hiring process.	Research school/district, initiatives, qualifications and criteria for hiring. Visit job posting sites.	Monitor job posting web sites.	Monitor job posting web sites for late summer openings.
Sep **Oct** **Nov**	**Dec** **Jan** **Feb**	**Mar** **Apr**	**May** **Jun-Jul-Aug**

List the types of schools, positions, and regions where you would like to teach. Consider different types of schools (e.g., public, independent, religious education, and other nonpublic) and teaching positions. Review the supply and demand chart by field and regions of the United States in the *AAEE Job Search Handbook for Educators*. This helpful tool makes it easy to locate the "high demand" geographical areas and teaching positions. Keep your doors open. **You will increase the chance of securing a teaching position if you're willing to expand your search beyond a 50-mile radius of your home community**.

Conduct a search for positions in "high demand" regions of the country. You will find more job openings where turnover is high such as high poverty urban areas or remote rural schools. There are more openings in the Southeast than New England. Search for positions at central job posting sites for different types of schools (e.g., public, independent, religious education, and other nonpublic), state departments of education, and career fairs. Monitor the sites for job openings from January-August.

If you earned a certification for a "low demand" teaching position, seek "high demand" endorsements. Earn endorsements in high demand areas such as special education, bilingual and English as a second language, math or science.

Before applying and interviewing, research your prospective school/district employer and their hiring process. Verify the required documents the school/district requires before submitting a complete application. Call the school district and ask who supervises the hiring and the application and interview process. Examine school/district web sites to understand the culture of the school community and the population of the students. The web sites can provide information about the curriculum, standards and assessment. Read about the school and district's

mission, current initiatives, the school board meeting minutes, and major issues they're facing. During the interview, use this information while answering questions.

Attend a school parent-teacher meeting. Schedule an observation of the school and classrooms prior to the interview. Walk the hallways. Observe arrival and dismissal of students. Notice wall hangings and posters that convey messages about the school.

The New Teachers Project (TNTP), a national nonprofit that works with low-performing schools to improve their hiring capacity, developed a hiring process. TNTP claims that teachers' character traits and leadership skills are the greatest determinants of their success. Seven selection criteria are: 1. critical thinking, 2. achievement, 3. personal responsibility, 4. commitment, 5. constant learning, 6. communication skills, and 7. etiquette.

The selection process begins with screening of all job seekers' written applications (e.g., background information, personal statement, transcript, résumé). Job seekers who show evidence of the above selection criteria are invited to a daylong interview conducted by trained principals and former principals. The interview can include a review of the candidate's résumé, personal statement, performance on a demonstration lesson, a proctored writing exercise, personal interview, and participation in a discussion group. Job-seekers must demonstrate evidence that they meet selection criteria to be recommended for acceptance.

Learn what employers value when selecting job applicants. In a recent survey, elementary principals ranked three selection factors as the most important selection factors for hiring: High level of verbal communication; high level of written communication; unique skills, knowledge and experience (Kniseley, 2009).

Important Selection Factors

Here are important selection factors used by principals for hiring recent graduates. The means (3 = high, 1 = low) are ranked from most important selection factor to least important selection factor. The ranking is based on responses from 35 elementary principals who were surveyed December 2008 - January 2009 (Kniseley, 2009).

IMPORTANT SELECTION FACTORS	MEAN
1. High level of verbal communication and interpersonal skills demonstrated during interviews or other meetings with the interview committee	2.91
2. High level of written communication demonstrated in application materials (e.g., application form, résumé, cover letter, on-site writing sample)	2.41
3. Unique skills, knowledge and experience (e.g., subject matter expertise, instructional technology, travel, prior professional experience)	2.37
4. Prior teaching experience (e.g., substitute teaching, full-time teaching in another school outside the district)	2.26
5. Direct observation of teaching by a member of the hiring committee (e.g., as part of interview, substitute teaching, student teaching)	2.21
6. A portfolio with clear evidence of effective teaching (e.g., binders or e-portfolios that includes evidence of planning, action, reflection)	2.20
7. Honors, awards, and recognition for teaching, scholarship, creativity, or community service	2.20
8. Strong letters of recommendation from applicant's references	2.14
9. Academic or teaching content major	2.09
10. Strong recommendations from applicant's references as part of a telephone background check	2.06
11. Endorsements beyond initial teaching certification (e.g., special education, ESL, middle level)	2.06
12. High grade point average on college/university transcript	1.97
13. Completion of an advanced degree (e.g., Master of Arts in Teaching, other post-graduate degree/certificate programs)	1.77
14. College/university where applicant completed his/her teacher education program	1.69

Recruitment, Application and Hiring

Schools and districts vary widely in the hiring process. And the hiring process differs for public school systems, charter, independent, and religious education schools. Before you submit your job application, research the school and district hiring process, application requirements, screening of applications, nature of the interview, and composition of the interview committee. Below are hiring processes used by two public school districts in Rhode Island.

PROVIDENCE PUBLIC SCHOOLS
Providence, the largest public school system in Rhode Island, includes 43 schools, two charter schools, 23,000 students, and 2,100 teachers.

Job Posting, Recruitment and Application Tracking System

Using an online application tracking system, job seekers search for jobs, post online profiles, submit applications, check the status of applications, and schedule interviews. There are no application deadlines. Providence utilizes a rolling application process where applicants are screened and interviewed as needed to fill teaching vacancies.

Criteria for Hiring

Seniority of teachers within the district is not the primary factor for selecting teachers for a vacancy. Teachers outside the system have an equal chance of landing a job in Providence. Qualified job applicants must be certified by State of Rhode Island in the appropriate area or endorsement. The interview committee assesses applicant knowledge and skills in five domains of effective teaching and five teacher competencies:

Selection Criteria (Five Domains of Effective Teaching)
* Knowledge of subjects and ability to teach them successfully
* Ability to create culturally and developmentally-appropriate lessons
* Ability to behave professionally as classroom managers, colleagues, and educational leaders for a diverse pool of learners
* Ability to utilize assessment data to guide instruction and plan for the future
* Ability to communicate well and knowledgeable about and committed to the extended school community

Five Teacher Competencies
* Content knowledge and pedagogy: expertise and success in teaching subject
* Achievement: shows a trend of excellence and concrete results in endeavors
* Critical thinking: analyzes situations thoroughly and generates effective strategies
* Communication skills: demonstrates effective written and oral skills
* Professional engagement: respectful of and sensitive to norms of interaction in different situations

Applicants create an online profile and upload résumés and essays. Applicants are encouraged to align the content of their résumés and essays to the selection criteria.
1. *Résumé:* Applicants list degrees earned, honors and awards, professional positions, responsibilities, and achievements.
2. *Essay:* Applicants share beliefs, methods, and achievements by responding to three writing prompts. The prompts relate to an applicant's knowledge and experience in raising students'

15

achievement levels, using data to drive decision-making about student support, and future plans for professional development. Applicants demonstrate mastery of English and critical thinking.

Three Written Essays

Applicants submit responses to three essays. Essays demonstrate the job applicant's best writing using aids such as dictionaries, books, the full capabilities of a word processor, and others who act as proofreaders.

When composing the essays, applicants communicate specific beliefs, methods, and achievements and relate to the five teacher competencies. They demonstrate mastery of English, mechanics of writing, critical thinking, and organization.

Here is a sample of a writing prompt.

> *Raising student achievement is the greatest challenge facing PPSD. Please explain what draws you to this work, what your academic and professional experiences will enable you to bring to it, and why you believe you will be successful in raising the achievement level of all your students.*

The Proctored Writing Sample

Prior to their scheduled interview, applicants complete a 30-minute, proctored writing sample. The writing sample represents the quality of writing without assistance or aids. The writing sample is similar to routine writing such as a parent communication.

When the applicant arrives, the proctor provides the applicant a writing prompt printed on a paper. Here is an example of a writing prompt:

> *Your school's state test scores were just released. Many of your current students achieved 'partially proficient.' You addressed your students' performance at recent parent/teacher conferences and want to follow-up with a letter.*
>
> *Write a letter to the parents of your students in which you share your plans for supporting the needs of your students across the remainder of the year. Be sure to provide parents with clear guidance about how they can support their children. Please feel free to invent any details you need to complete the scenario.*

Applicants use a computer that displays a text box, provides word processing functionality and a minute-by-minute countdown of the remaining time. No aids are permitted such as dictionaries, paper, writing instruments, notes, computers, electronic devices, and printed materials.

The Interview

The hiring committee interviews the finalists for about 60 minutes. The committee uses interview questions from a common bank of questions and concrete teaching scenarios. Here are some classroom management scenarios:

- High School: *A student has a crush on you and exhibits inappropriate behavior by flirting and physically leaning on you. What do you do next?*
- Middle School: *Two students with good academic records begin shoving each other just before you begin to teach a lesson. What do you do next?*
- Elementary School: *While conferencing with a small group of students, a sobbing, distressed student suddenly leaves the room without following the class rules of signing out and taking a hall pass. What do you do next?*

The Demonstration Lesson

Each applicant is required to teach a 15-20 minute lesson to the committee. During the interview, the committee assesses the applicant's knowledge and skills: *Does the candidate know his/her subject? Can the candidate demonstrate knowledge of recent research in his/her discipline? Is the candidate able to demonstrate his/her knowledge within the model lesson?*

Screening Applicants

The human resources department screens all of the application packets and selects those meeting minimum requirements. Approved applications are forwarded to level directors and principals who use rating sheets to evaluate the quality of job applications. They call the applicants who are recommended for interviewing.

Composition of the Interview Committee

The school-based interview committee includes the principal, two teachers selected by the principal, two teachers selected by the School Improvement Team, and a department head at the high school level. Members of the interview committee are trained to select teachers using a hiring process developed by The New Teachers Project.

Final Decisions

Using the criteria, interview committee members score each job applicant and recommend to the principal up to six job applicants with the highest total scores. The principal ranks the job applicants with the top three scores 1-3 (in any order) and then ranks alternates in any order starting with 4. The principal makes the final decision although their judgment should reflect the consensus of the committee. After the interview, applicants complete an online questionnaire and indicate which school they prefer. The successful applicant's preference of schools is matched to the decision of the interview committee.

WARWICK PUBLIC SCHOOLS
Warwick Public Schools, the second largest school system in Rhode Island, includes 25 schools, 10,000 students, and 900 teachers.

Job Posting, Recruitment and Applying for Positions
The district recruits applicants by advertising in the *Sunday Providence Journal* classified ads and at teacher job fairs. There is no application deadline. Vacancies are filled as needed. Vacancies are posted at the district human resources web site.

The application includes the following:
- Application form
- Résumé
- Graduate and undergraduate transcripts showing degrees conferred and date. A copy is acceptable. For student teachers, a copy of their transcripts through their most recent, completed semester is acceptable until degree conferred
- Three written letters of reference
- Copy of Rhode Island or Northeast Regional Certificate teacher certificate. If currently a teacher education student, a student teaching certificate is acceptable.
- Copy of scores from state certification or licensing test, PLT, NTE or Praxis exam

Initial Screening
The human resources department screens all applications and selects applicants who meet the minimum requirements for the position such as appropriate certifications and endorsements, degrees, and course work. A "student teaching certificate" will suffice until the applicant receives an official document from the state department of education. Next, the human resources representative phones qualified applicants and schedules the applicant for an interview. Then, application materials are forwarded to the interview committee.

Composition of the Interview Committee
The interview committee consists of 3-5 people and includes administrators, department heads, principals, teachers or a human resources department representative. For elementary teaching positions, the committee includes elementary principals. For middle, secondary, special education and other specialist teaching positions, the committee includes administrators, department heads, principals, teachers or a human resources representative.

The Interview
The interview committee conducts a 30-minute interview with finalists. Interview questions focus on experience, philosophy of education, knowledge of teaching, experience with classroom management, differentiated instruction, academic progress and extra curricular involvement. The committee submits notes and recommendations of finalists to human resources department and the director of elementary, secondary, or special education.

Final Decision

The director of elementary, secondary or special education recommends a finalist for a vacant position to the superintendent.

The New Teachers Project Selection Process

The New Teacher Project (Daly and Kramer, 2007) found that teachers' character traits and leadership skills are the greatest determinants of their success. The selection process begins with the screening of all job applicants' written applications (e.g., background information, personal statement, transcript, résumé). Job applicants who show evidence of the selection criteria are invited to a daylong interview conducted by trained selectors including principals and former principals. The interview includes a review of the job applicant's résumé, personal statement, performance on a demonstration lesson, a writing exercise, personal interview, and participation in a discussion group. Successful job applicants demonstrate evidence that they meet or exceed selection criteria.

SELECTION CRITERIA

Critical Thinking

Analyzes situations thoroughly and generates effective strategies

• Discerns the presence and nature of problems accurately
• Develops creative solutions
• Displays logical approach to all situations

Achievement

Shows a trend of excellence in endeavors and focuses on concrete results

• Strong academic record that warrants admission to a rigorous course of study and/or has surpassed employer expectations in previous positions
• Has set and met ambitious goals
• Takes on challenges

Personal Responsibility

Assumes accountability for reaching outcomes despite obstacles

• Focuses on own capacity to impact situations rather than on external barriers
• Maintains bigger picture perspective when confronted with setbacks
• Takes initiative to solve own problems

Commitment

Committed to raising academic achievement in high need schools

• Desire to work in a community with high need schools
• Believes that students of all backgrounds can and must learn at high levels

Constant Learning
Draws lessons from previous experiences and applies them to future endeavors
• Reflects regularly on performance to identify areas of improvement
• Seeks and welcomes feedback from others
• Accesses resources to support self-development

Communication Skills
Demonstrates effective written and oral skills
• Displays mastery of written grammar, usage, and organization
• Speaks clearly and precisely
• Fluent verbal and written command of English

Etiquette
• Demonstrates professional behavior and attire

Getting Your Foot in the Door - Substitute Teach!

Employers say substitute teaching is a great way to get your foot in the door. You can network with principals and teachers and check out the wide range of schools. Some districts guarantee substitute teachers an interview for a full-time teaching position if they substitute teach in the district for a specific period of time.

When teaching, invite the principal to observe you teach. A positive teaching performance can lead to an interview. Take time to build relationships with the faculty and staff. Arrive early to review the teacher's daily lesson plans and other instructions. Introduce yourself to the clerks, custodians, teachers and principal. "Good morning, I'm Albert Einstein and I am subbing for Ms. McClintock today. Nice to meet you!" During your lunchtime, eat your meal in the faculty room.

At the end of the day, write notes summarizing what you taught and any problems you encountered with specific students. End the note with a "thank you." Hopefully, you can compliment the teacher for leaving excellent instructions and lesson plans and a well-managed classroom. In any event, leave a positive message. Before you depart, spruce up the classroom. Leave the teacher's desk neater than found.

The district hiring process for substitute teaching differs. Some districts require you to apply online for substitute teaching at teacher recruitment web sites. Other districts require you to submit printed application materials to the director of human resources.

One district requires the following application materials for substitute teaching:
• Completed job application
• Résumé

- Two forms of I.D.
- Copy of transcript
- Three letters of recommendation
- Copy of your Praxis II scores
- Copy of your Professional Teacher Certification (or Student Teaching Certification)
- Documentation by a physician that you are free of tuberculosis (TB) and measles-mumps-rubella (MMR) in its communicable form.

Typically, applicants meet with the director of human resources for an interview and a review of application materials. If successful, the director requests that you complete a federal background check for a criminal record. Then, the director places you in the district substitute teaching pool for day-to-day substitute teaching and/or long-term substitute positions.

Advice from a Human Resources Department Representative

Here is advice from a veteran human resource department representative who screens applicants and works with interview committees (personal communication with Ms. Shannon Sweeney Saunders, Warwick Public Schools):

Job Search
- Incorporate substitute teaching as a strategy for getting a full-time position. You can network and compare schools and districts. You can increase your chances of getting a job by entering the substitute teaching pool and earning endorsements in middle school and special education. Individuals who are substitute teachers will usually be called for an interview. Although we don't guarantee an interview, we usually interview all of our substitute teachers.
- When applying for jobs, be strategic. Don't spread yourself too thin. Submit applications in a variety of districts, but not all districts.
- Only apply for jobs for which you're qualified.
- Read and follow the job application instructions carefully. Do not omit any parts.

Transcripts
- When reviewing transcripts, it's understood that applicants may have low GPAs at the beginning of their college program. What's important is evidence of progression towards a higher GPA.

Résumés
- Develop a résumé that is clear and easy to read. Indicate your teaching certifications and endorsements. Arrange your work experience chronologically. Indicate other experiences with students outside of the workday such as coaching, work at Boys and Girls Clubs, and volunteer work.

Interviewing
- Bring your résumé and list of references. You can bring a hiring portfolio to an interview containing items that might relate to any interview question. However, it's not required. Include items that might set you apart from others. What makes you more outstanding than the other one hundred who are applying for the position? Prepare to direct the attention of your interviewers to one component serving as evidence or helping to explain your knowledge and experience.
- Use teacher job fairs as an opportunity to practice interviewing and to increase your awareness of teaching opportunities in other school systems in the region or other parts of the United States.

References
- For recent graduates, letters of recommendations are preferred from your cooperating teacher, college supervisor of student teaching, and the principal at your student teaching site.

Advice from a School Administrator

Here is advice from a middle school assistant principal with many years of experience hiring teachers (personal communication with Mr. Daniel Smith, Feinstein Middle School, Coventry RI):

Applications and Hiring Process
- Read the qualifications for the position carefully in the job posting. Don't apply if you aren't qualified. Understand the requirements and qualifications stated in the job description for the specific position before you customize and submit job application materials.
- Research the school and district. Know the school mission, initiatives, curriculum, and standards. Find out who is on the interviewing committee and who supervises the hiring process. After you submit your application, email the supervisor and inform him/her that you have submitted an online application.
- Initially, the cover letter, résumé, and references are reviewed quickly to see if the job applicant meets the qualifications. These items are reviewed more carefully when selecting finalists for interview. When selecting finalists, references are contacted for further information.

Cover Letters and Résumés
- Your cover letter should grab the readers' attention. Personalize the content. The content should not read like a textbook. Relate your letter to the specific job description, qualifications, school mission and initiatives.
- Promote your strengths but don't exaggerate. WRONG: I single-handedly turned the school from a low performing school to a high performing school.
- Vary the use of action verbs. Use a thesaurus. There is no tolerance for errors in spelling, grammar, and punctuation. Ask a skilled writer to proofread your cover letter.

- Before inserting a cover letter and résumé into an online teacher recruitment site, word-process offline and proofread carefully.
- Be prepared in the interview to explain the reasons for the gaps in your experience or reasons for leaving a position. When addressing gaps or non-education experiences, explain how these life skills strengthen your classroom teaching.
- For your résumé, emphasize relevant knowledge, skills, and dispositions. Relate to the specific job description, qualifications, school mission and initiatives. Include professional memberships. Include relevant professional development experiences.

References
- Select three to five references. Include your cooperating teacher and college supervisor.
- Include personal contact numbers and email since calls are often made during the summer and teachers/professors who may not be available at the school number.

Interviewing
- To gauge the length of your responses, ask the human resources department representative how long the interview will be and the number of questions. Ask for sample questions.
- Get to know the school. Before the day of the interview, visit the school, walk the hallways and observe teaching.
- Show up at the school 30 minutes before the scheduled interview. Wait in your car and walk in five to ten minutes early.
- Dress appropriately.
- Answer questions thoroughly and succinctly.
- Remember: You're interviewing the school as well. Ask questions to demonstrate knowledge of school and district initiatives and what is valued. *How is your advisory program working? What challenges are you facing?* Ask questions about school and district needs that you have identified from your research.
- Prepare a model lesson if that is part of the interview process. And, of course, this is not the time to wing it!
- Demonstrate courtesy throughout. Keep the doors open.

Portfolios
- Select eight to ten items – your "best of best work." Use current educational terms.
- Refer to leading theorists.
- Use the portfolio during the interview as a source of examples.

Advice from Recent Graduates

Here is advice from recent Rhode Island College graduates who won teaching positions shortly after graduation.

- Be confident. Believe in yourself. When I interviewed, I would tell myself things like "You deserve this job!" With higher confidence, you are able to deliver knowledgeable answers with more conviction.

- Preparation is important! To prepare for the interview, I made 100 note cards based on the most common questions asked. I developed what I thought were perfect answers and studied them every day. I studied the Title 1 laws and program intensely. I set up two mock interviews with teachers who I have worked with in the past.

- Use an online job-posting site when looking for jobs. That is how I got all of my interviews.

- Have an open mind. When you apply for a job, cast a wide search net. I would have loved a job in my home state, but I am teaching full-time four hours away and I love it.

- I'm teaching full-time as a special education teacher in a middle school - an hour from my home. Be open to travelling an hour to work at a job in your field.

- I didn't get hired after my first interview, my second or my third. But I never gave up hope. My long-term sub position began in October and has been extended to March. I took on a big school-home book bags project, differentiating instruction and just conducted my first IEP meeting. I have been updating my portfolio and adding teaching experience to my résumé.

- Don't expect to get your dream job right away. I have many peers who refuse to take subbing or short-term jobs and they are not gaining any experience in their fields. I am subbing, and though it's not my dream job, I am gaining experience and taking steps toward a better career.

- To increase your opportunity (if living in a small state), get a teacher certificates in nearby states. Add endorsements beyond initial certification to make you more marketable.

Hot Topics for Schools and Districts

Get familiar with the hot topics facing your future employer. Below are a list of 20 major issues facing schools and districts. While you research the school or district, narrow the list to a manageable number.

1. Educational reform – "Race to the Top"
2. Common core standards
3. Accountability: Using assessment data for planning improvement of teaching and learning
4. Closing the achievement gap: Raising achievement levels of low-performing students and schools
5. High stakes assessment and teacher evaluation
6. Teacher quality
7. Special education law; parental rights; individual education plans; response to intervention
8. English language learners
9. Parent involvement
10. Reading and writing - early intervention and adolescent literacy
11. Math and science – problem-solving and hands on, inquiry learning
12. Teaching for understanding – "Understanding by Design" (ASCD)
13. Universal Design for Learning (CAST)
14. Middle school concept – advising, cooperative learning, integrated learning
15. Extended school day and year
16. Out of school programming
17. High school retention and dropout
18. STEM (Science, Technology, Engineering, Mathematics)
19. 21st Century classrooms; integrating instructional technology
20. Bullying and teasing

Compose a Résumé and Cover Letter

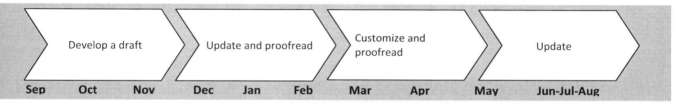

Develop a 2-page résumé by following these steps:

1. Brainstorm a list of your knowledge, skills, and dispositions related to effective teaching.
2. Briefly describe your behaviors and accomplishments – relate to specific teaching experiences (e.g., coursework, student teaching, other teaching). Use the language of the profession.
3. Select items relevant to the teaching position or knowledge, skills, dispositions, and accomplishments that set you apart from others.
4. Create résumé components.
   - Your name
   - Contact information
   - Objective
   - Education with GPA
   - Honors and awards
   - Education experience
   - Related work experience
   - Community/volunteer activities
   - Interests/extracurricular activities
   - References (with contact information)

Some teacher recruitment sites allow you to add custom résumé and cover letter sections. Be sure to take advantage of this feature.

A well-written résumé and cover letter will help you pass the initial screening. Upon receiving job application materials, screeners read a résumé and notice whether the applicant meets minimum qualifications such as a required degree, state certifications, and required skills. Initially, an employer skims a résumé in 30 seconds or less. Next, the reader quickly reviews the skills-based action verb descriptions under Education Experience and Related Work Experiences. If this portion of the résumé catches the employers' attention, they are more likely to go back and read the résumé and the cover letter more carefully. If you make the cut, the interviewing committee examines the résumé to see what makes you unique and/or more qualified than other finalists. Developing a résumé also prepares you mentally for a clear response to interview questions such as, *Tell us about your background. Why are you a good fit for this position at this time?*

The cover letter introduces you to employers, grabs their attention, increases their interest, and convinces them that you are the person to hire.

Develop a one-page cover letter with these essential components:

- Address the letter to a particular individual in the district. If that person is not apparent, call the district office for that person's name and title.
- *Paragraph 1:* State that you are interested in applying to that particular school and district and that you are qualified for the position (degree, content major, etc.) and have the required certifications and endorsements. Relate your strengths to the qualifications.
- *Paragraph 2:* Be enthusiastic and demonstrate that you have researched the district and school and how hiring you will benefit the school/district (e.g., relevant knowledge, related experiences, essential skills, how your philosophy is aligned with the school/district mission).
- *Paragraph 3:* Request an interview and include your phone number and email address in your closing paragraph.
- Sign your letter (if applicable) and check that your contact information is plainly visible.

Carefully format and proofread your résumé and cover. There is no tolerance for poor written communication. Ask a skilled writer to proofread it.

Developing Your Résumé

Here are three steps:

Step 1 - List and briefly describe your activities.

List all experiences:

— *Education* (List your teacher education program and content major/teaching concentration, and endorsement programs.)
— *Prior employment related to teaching* (e.g., dance teacher, professional tutor, summer camp counselor, group home counselor),
— *Practical teaching* (e.g., practicum, student teaching)
— *Community service/volunteer activities* (e.g., tutoring, summer camp, coaching sports and cheerleading, Girl/Boy Scout leader, museum docent, parent-teacher organization, school improvement team, Habitat for Humanity, Food Bank)
— *Skill/knowledge development beyond course work related to career of teaching* [e.g., instructional technology, classroom management, second language (Spanish is especially important in urban districts.), leadership, public speaking]
— *Leadership* (e.g., officer in student organization, volunteer organization, sports team, PTO)
— *Member of relevant professional/pre-professional organizations* (e.g., Future Elementary and Early Childhood Teachers, Middle Level Association, NSTA Chapter for Students)
— *Unique interests/activities* (e.g., varsity/inter-collegiate sports, study abroad experiences, world travel, web design, fund-raising events for charity such as the MS 150 Bike Tour)
— *Honors and awards* (e.g., scholarships, department awards, leadership awards)

Step 2 - Select items relevant to the teaching position.

"Relevant" means relevant practicum and student teaching experiences, volunteer/community service activities, and recognition – honors and awards. List them individually, chronologically – most recent first. Include grade, subject, school and district, units taught or content-skills developed by your students, and major achievements.

Step 3 - Create résumé components.

Include work experiences if relevant to the teaching position and/or the experiences that have helped you develop the knowledge and skills needed for varied teaching roles and duties (e.g., collaboration, leadership, working with diverse populations). Include military, AmeriCorps, City Year, or Peace Corps service experiences.

If you haven't completed the student teaching semester, include the expected date of completion. Unless you're applying for a teaching position in an independent or religious education school, you will not get beyond the screening phase for public school teaching positions without the necessary credentials.

Use official titles of state certifications. For example,

- State of Rhode Island Elementary Teacher Professional Certificate

- State of Rhode Island Special Educator – Elementary and Middle Level Professional Certificate
- State of Rhode Island Middle Level Endorsement

Promote your strengths but don't exaggerate the results. (WRONG: "I single-handedly raised the per cent of students' passing the state mathematics assessment from 23% to 93%.")

Be careful about explaining gaps in employment and education. For the interview, prepare to explain reasons for gaps or leaving a position. If possible, address gaps by explaining how these life skills strengthen your classroom teaching.

Format and proofread your job application materials carefully. Use high-level written communication. Vary the action verbs. Use a thesaurus. There is zero tolerance for errors in spelling, grammar, and punctuation. If applying online, word-process your documents offline and proofread carefully before inserting them into the online application. Ask a highly skilled writer to proofread your work.

How Employers Read a Résumé

Initially, an employer skims a résumé in less than a minute. Employers notice if the applicant meets minimum qualifications such a required degree, state certifications, and required skills.

The "Career Objective" component provides a brief way to communicate to the employer the position to which position you are applying. It frames how the employer considers the information that follows the objective: Do the education, related experiences, and skills support the objective? An objective is a one-line phrase, such as:

> CAREER OBJECTIVE: *To teach as a general education elementary teacher in an urban school setting*

Next, the employer quickly reviews the skills-based, action verb descriptions under "Student Teaching and Practicum" and "Related Work Experiences" that are most critical to supporting a job seeker's application. If this component of the résumé catches the employer's attention, they are more likely to go back and carefully read the résumé and the cover letter.

Templates for Résumés

Here are three templates recommended by Rhode Island College Career Development Center:

Template 1

NAME_____

Street, town, state, zip   phone, email

OBJECTIVE (Be specific about position your are seeking.)

EDUCATION
        Rhode Island College, Providence, RI
        B.S./B.A. in Elementary Education, expected year
        GPA (if 3.0 or higher)

        Certifications: (if applicable – e.g., CPR)

        Knowledge of (list specific computer skills)
        Fluent in ….; proficient in …. (list languages along with levels of proficiency)

CERTIFICATIONS
        State
        Professional Certificate
        Endorsement

EDUCATION EXPERIENCE

Student Teaching
        SCHOOL, location   Semester/Year
- Action verb
- Action verb

Practicum (list all)   Semester/Year
        Subject - Field. SCHOOL, Location

ADDITIONAL EXPERIENCE (Include experiences such as tutoring, summer camps.)

Organization, Location. Title.   Dates

COMMUNITY/VOLUNTEER   Dates

INTERESTS/EXTRA CURRICULAR ACTIVITIES

References available upon request.

Template 2

NAME
Street, town, state, zip   phone, email

OBJECTIVE (Be specific about position you are seeking.)

EDUCATION

     Rhode Island College, Providence, RI
     B.S./B.A. in Elementary Education, expected year
     GPA (if 3.0 or higher)

     Other College attended, Location
     Degree, date or years attended

     Knowledge of (List specific computer skills.)
     Fluent in ….; proficient in …. (List languages and levels of proficiency.)

CERTIFICATIONS
     State
     Professional Certificate
     Endorsement

EDUCATION EXPERIENCE

     SCHOOL/ORGANIZATION   Location
     Title   Dates
- Action verb (Use as many as needed to identify relevant skills.)
- Action verb
- Action verb

     SCHOOL/ORGANIZATION   Location
     Title   Dates
- Action verb
- Action verb
- Action verb

     Title (if you've held more than one position with this firm)   Dates
- Action verb
- Action verb
- Action verb

ADDITIONAL EXPERIENCE
     ORGANIZATION   Location
     Title   Dates

References available upon request.

Template 3 – With Pre-Student Teaching Practicum Experiences

NAME
Street, town, state, zip   phone, email

OBJECTIVE (Be specific about position you are seeking.)

EDUCATION
      Rhode Island College, Providence, RI
      B.S./B.A. in Elementary Education, expected year
      GPA (if 3.0 or higher)

      Other College attended, Location
      Degree, date or years attended

      Knowledge of (List specific computer skills.)
      Fluent in ….; proficient in …. (List languages and levels of proficiency.)

CERTIFICATIONS
      State
      Professional Certificate
      Endorsement

EDUCATION EXPERIENCE

Student Teaching
      SCHOOL, location   Sem/Year
        • Action verb
        • Action verb

Practicum Experiences: Elementary Education   Sem/Year
• ELED 422 Developmental Reading and Writing: *Balanced Literacy,* School, Location
• ELED 438 Mathematics: Investigations: School, Location
• ELED 437 Science: *FOSS Earth Materials:* School, Location
• ELED 435 Reading: *Reading Street Program* School, Location
• ELED 436 Social Studies: School, Location

Practicum Experiences: Special Education (minimum of 30 hours in each)   Sem/Year
• SPED 300 Introduction to Special Education: School, Location.
• SPED 301 Behavior Modification, Speech and Language Disorders: School, Location
• SPED 302 Assessments for Special Education Students: School, Location

ORGANIZATION   Location
      Title   Dates
        • Action verb
        • Action verb

ADDITIONAL EXPERIENCE
Organization   Location
      Title   Dates

References available upon request.

Criteria for Effective Teaching Résumés

Here is a checklist developed by Rhode Island College's Career Development Center and modified by the author.

APPEARANCE

___ is inviting and easy to read
___ uses appropriate font styles and font sizes (10 –14 pts.)
___ incorporates enough "white "space" between sections to emphasize key works
___ print is letter quality
___ appropriate length (ideally no more than two pages)

WRITING STYLE

___ begins sentences or phrases with powerful action verbs ("scannable" résumés require nouns)
___ short paragraphs mostly under five lines; short sentences/phrases
___ brief, succinct language; no unnecessary words
___ free from grammatical, spelling, punctuation, usage and typographical errors

CONTENT

Contact Information:

___ mailing address (current and permanent if necessary)
___ telephone number (where you can be reached or a message left from 9 am to 5 pm)
___ email address

Objective

___ briefly indicates position sought – may use actual title and area of specialization
___ language is specific, employer-centered, avoids broad or vague statements

Education

___ highest level of attainment is listed first; work in reverse chronological order
___ degree in progress or most recently completed degree; include name and location of college, type of degree, "candidate for" or "awarded"
___ list other degrees; relevant higher education coursework, continuing professional education or training courses and studies abroad
___ major(s), minor(s), program(s)
___ omit high school
___ GPA (if 3.0 or higher), honors, department and leadership awards, scholarships
___ percentage of educational expenses earned (through off-campus employment, work study)

Certification

___ includes certification with date
  o State of Rhode Island Elementary Teacher Professional Certificate (Expected May 2010)
  o State of Rhode Island Special Educator – Elementary and Middle Level Professional Certificate (Expected May 2010)
  o State of Rhode Island Middle Level Endorsement (Expected May 2010)

Education Experience

Include all formal education or paid work experiences (teacher education program, teacher assistant) that are relevant to your objective. Start with the most recent experience and work in reverse chronological order.

___ title held, school name, city, state (e.g. Full Semester Student Teacher, Student Teacher, and Teacher Assistant). Include grade level and content area.

___ dates position held (if several positions for same employer – list employer once and put titles and job descriptions in reverse chronological order. e.g., Fall Semester 2010; Spring Semester 2009)

___ indicates transferable skills and adaptive abilities used in job – what problems did you solve?

___ contribution to organizations – ways your work improved quality of programs, communication (e.g., organized Family Math Night; developed newsletter to parents/families; developed and maintained classroom web page; served as judge for Senior Projects)

___ quantitative or qualitative indicators that describe results of your contributions or accomplishments, e.g., "improved sight word vocabulary of students from X to X."

___ learning that took place on job that is relevant to your job objective (learned to implement Reading Street program; trained to use SMART Board technology; trained by district to administer NECAP mathematics assessments; attended professional development on backwards design approach to unit planning called *Understanding by Design;* participated in IEP and RTI meetings)

___ If applicable, include service in military, AmeriCorps, City Year, or Peace Corps.

Additional Experience: Extra-Curricular Activities and Community Service

___ significant positions of responsibility; include title, name of organization or team, dates

___ leadership roles, achievements (e.g., officer in student organization, volunteer organization, sports team, PTO)

___ memberships to pre- professional education organizations (e.g., Future Elementary And Early Childhood Teachers, Middle Level Association, RIC Chapter of NSTA)

___ volunteer activities (e.g., tutoring, summer camp, coaching sports and cheerleading, Girl/Boy Scout leader, museum docent, parent-teacher organization, school improvement team, Habitat for Humanity, RI Food Bank)

Related Skills

___ computer skills; software applications, languages, hardware, operating systems; specify level of competence – "novice," "proficient," "expert"

___ foreign language skills; specify level of fluency and ability to read and write as "basic," "working knowledge," "proficient, " "fluent," or "bilingual"

___ leadership development; grant-writing skills

___ skill of working with diverse populations

OVERALL EFFECTIVENESS

___ demonstrates ability or potential to do the job; supports your career objective, speaks to the employer's needs and requirements (employer-centered)

___ indicates knowledge of field, typical issues or problems, solutions

___ omits age, gender, marital, status, names of references

Composing a Cover Letter

Treat the cover letter as a marketing tool. Sell yourself well. Build the case for the employer to hire you.

Customize a one-page, four-paragraph, standard business letter that relates your knowledge of teaching, skills, experience, and commitment to the specific job qualifications.

Paragraph 1

Begin the letter by stating that you are pleased to apply for the specific job (state title and reference number from the source of job posting). Also state that you meet the qualifications for the position and hold the required teaching certificate/endorsement (exact title and state), degree and major.

Paragraph 2

Next, explain why hiring you will benefit the school/district and its students. Relate to the school mission and initiatives. For example, if you are applying for a teaching position in an urban district with low-performing schools, emphasize your knowledge and experience of working with urban youth and families, what you can do personally to work with others in the school to raise student achievement of all learners, and how you have used assessment information in decision-making. If available, address the criteria used for hiring.

Paragraph 3

Then, explain what makes you unique as a job applicant. Highlight several personal strengths related to the job qualifications and mission of the school district.

Paragraph 4

Thank the employer for considering your application. Express confidence in your abilities and that you are highly qualified for the position. Provide your telephone number to schedule an interview or follow-up. Indicate enclosures such as a résumé, application form or other attachments.

Written Communication

Since cover letters are used for screening purposes, many employers desire succinct, one-page cover letters that are easy to read. Do not repeat all of the details of your résumé.

Format the letter as a standard business letter (e.g., block, modified block, semi-block). Use single-spaces. Double-space between paragraphs.

Use high-level written communication. Express enthusiasm and commitment. Vary the action verbs. Use a thesaurus. Proofread carefully. There is zero tolerance for errors in spelling, grammar, and punctuation.

If you are composing a cover letter for an online teacher recruitment site, then word process offline. Ask a highly skilled writer to proofread your work. Then insert into the application.

Criteria For Effective Cover Letters
Here is a checklist developed by Rhode Island College's Career Development Center and modified by the author.

APPEARANCE
> __ inviting and easy to read
> __ print is letter quality; looks professional

ORGANIZATION AND FORMAT
> __ purpose of letter is immediately clear
> __ paragraph organization has logic and sequence as indicated by appropriate topic sentences
> __ most important job relevant facts placed first
> __ one page, 3 to 4 paragraphs
> __ utilizes standard business letter format (e.g., block, modified block, semi-block)
> __ main elements of business letter: date, inside address, salutation, body, complimentary close, signature, and typed name are present and follow business letter rules
> __ single-spaced (double-spaced between paragraphs)

WRITING STYLE
> __ clear, concise, readable, catches reader's attention
> __ tone expresses enthusiasm and energy; is warm, positive, and professional
> __ uses short, concrete familiar words
> __ avoids inappropriate jargon, clichés, and trite phrases
> __ uses concrete facts and evidence to demonstrate competence ("I received an award as 'employee of the month' for my customer relations work"), not subjective, self-praise ("I have superb customer relations skills")
> __ No errors in grammar, spelling, punctuation

CONTENT
Paragraph One
> __ identifies reason for writing (e.g. applying for a specific job, request for information interview, thank you for interview, accepting offer)
> __ indicates where, when, and how you learned about the job
> __ identifies you by one or more descriptors: profession, degree, experience, school, and date of graduation, or relationship to person referring you
> __ may indicate your interest in and knowledge of the organization

Paragraph Two
> __ leads with statement indicating you have the qualifications needed to meet the employer's requirements and the job and/or that you can add value to the organization (even if you lack some qualifications and experience)
> __ convinces the reader by introducing factual evidence to support your qualifications
> __ elaborates on your strongest qualifications that match employer requirements

__ gives concise overview of your work history in relationship to job requirements

__ provides concrete examples of job related accomplishments or results obtained through work, school, extracurricular activities, or volunteer work

__ illustrates what you achieved or learned from experiences listed on résumé – not merely what you did

__ may indicate types of problems you can solve (for experienced job-seekers)

Paragraph Three (optional)

__ convinces the reader by providing further evidence of your qualifications, personal qualities, knowledge, strengths, goals, interests, skills, academic experience, and accomplishments

__ may provide evidence of benefits you can offer (for experienced job-seekers)

Paragraph Four

__ indicates enclosures, attachments

__ expresses confidence in your abilities

__ indicates how you may be reached during regular business hours

__ indicates when you will telephone to schedule an interview or to follow-up

__ thanks the employer for considering your request

MARKETING FOCUS

__ demonstrates ability or potential to do the job and meet employer's requirements

__ shows awareness of employer's needs/challenges/problems

__ indicates knowledge of school, district, initiatives, field, challenges, and issues

__ omits extraneous information unrelated to position, employer needs, or your qualifications

Example of a Simple Résumé

Albert Einstein
160 Genius Blvd.
Princeton, NJ 08542
(609) 345-6789
aeinstein@njc.edu

OBJECTIVE	To teach Grades 1-6 elementary education

EDUCATION

New Jersey College   May 22, 2010
B.A. in Elementary Education
Content Major in Science
GPA: 3.7/4.0, Dean's List for 6 semesters

Honors and Awards:
- Department of Elementary Education Award
- Sir Isaac Newton Science Scholarship

Related Skills:
- Proficient user of Microsoft Office (Word, Excel and PowerPoint), Front Page (web design), SMART Board, and document cameras. Novice user of classroom response systems and Tablet PC
- Fluent in Spanish

CERTIFICATION   **State of New Jersey Elementary Professional Teacher**   May 2010

EDUCATION EXPERIENCE

Stadium School, Cranston NJ   Spring 2010
Full-Semester Student Teaching, Grade 1
- Differentiated instruction to accommodate diverse learners
- Developed and implemented an integrated thematic unit using *Reading Street Program*
- Attended open house, parent conferences, faculty and grade level common plan time meetings, and IEP- RTI meetings
- Implemented class and individual behavior management programs

Washington Oak School, Coventry, NJ   Fall 2009
Science Practicum, Grade 4
- Team planned and taught a 4th grade a hands on, inquiry science unit aligned with Common Core Standards in Science using Lawrence Hall of Science FOSS *Earth Materials* science module
- Incorporated scientist notebooks to improve scientific thinking and communication
- Developed the unit using the *Understanding by Design* "backwards design approach" in a 3^{rd}grade inclusion classroom

Mary Fogarty School, Providence, NJ   Spring 2009
Social Studies Practicum, Grade 5
- Team planned and implemented a 5th grade social studies unit on
- Rhode Island history using primary sources and children's historical fiction
- Planned a historical walking field trip with the NJ Historical Society

Charles Fortes School, Providence, NJ   Fall 2008
Mathematics Practicum, Grade 4
- Conducted a 4th grade problem-solving unit aligned with NJGLEs in Mathematics using TERC *Investigations*
- Created and implemented a unit plan and all corresponding lessons with accommodations and modifications for students with special needs

RELATED EXPERIENCE

New Jersey College *Study Abroad Program*   January 2009
- Traveled to England for three weeks to learn about Great Britain's teacher education programs and national curriculum
- Observed and taught lessons in three different primary schools and attended classes at the University of Cumbria in Carlisle, England

Audubon Society of New Jersey, Bristol NJ   2006-2008
Teacher Assistant. ASNJ Environmental Education Program
- Planned and assisted ASNJ Director of Education with school field trips to the Environmental Education Center and visits to school classrooms.

COMMUNITY/ VOLUNTEER

Tutor, Inspiring Minds (formerly Volunteers in Providence Schools)   Spring 2009
Carpenter, Habitat for Humanity – New Orleans, LA   Spring 2008
Fund-Raiser and Cyclist, NJ MS 150 Bike Tour   June 2007

EXTRACUR- RICULAR ACTIVITIES/ INTERESTS

Treasurer, NJC's Future Elementary Teachers   2009-present
Member, NJC's Student Chapter, National Science Teachers Assoc.   2008-present
Interests: fitness, digital photography, travel, reading science fiction

References Available Upon Request

Example of a Résumé With Sidebars – Quotes from References

Albert Einstein
160 Genius Blvd.
Princeton, NJ 08542
(609) 345-6789
aeinstein@njc.edu

One of the best students I have supervised in 15 years ….a rising star! - Barbara McClintock, Cooperating Teacher	**OBJECTIVE:** To teach Grades 1-6 elementary education

OBJECTIVE: To teach Grades 1-6 elementary education

EDUCATION: **New Jersey College**
B.A. in Elementary Education   May 22, 2010
Content Major in Science
GPA: 3.7/4.0, Dean's List

CERTIFICATION State of New Jersey Elementary Professional Teacher
      May 2010

STUDENT TEACHING & PRACTICUM EXPERIENCE:

Sidebar: One of the best students I have supervised in 15 years ….a rising star!
- Barbara McClintock, Cooperating Teacher

Stadium School, Cranston NJ   Spring 2010
<u>Full semester student teaching</u>
- Differentiated instruction to accommodate diverse learners
- Developed and implemented an integrated thematic unit using a hands on Lawrence Hall of Science science module called FOSS *Balance and Motion*
- Attended open house, parent conferences, faculty and grade level common plan time meetings, and IEP- RTI meetings
- Implemented class and individual behavior management programs

Sidebar: Albert will be able to mentor your veteran teachers! At the beginning of his field placement, Albert learned to use the school's SmartBoard and creatively integrated the technology in all of his lessons. He presented a workshop to faculty who had never used the SMART Board.
- Robert Oppenheimer, Principal

Washington Oak School, Coventry, NJ   Fall 2009
<u>Science methods</u>
- Team planned and taught a 4th grade a hands on, inquiry science unit aligned with Common Core Standards in Science using Lawrence Hall of Science FOSS *Earth Materials* science module
- Incorporated scientist notebooks to improve scientific thinking
- Developed the unit using the *Understanding by Design* "backwards design approach"

Sidebar: I was impressed with how Albert established rapport with students so quickly. On the first day he could call students by their first names. He related to each student's talents, interests, and learning needs.
- Niels Bohr, College Supervisor

Elizabeth Baldwin School, Pawtucket, NJ   Spring 2009
Reading and language arts methods
- Implemented guided reading lessons to a group of five students with special needs in a 3rd grade inclusion classroom
- Administered diagnostic, formative and summative assessments

Mary Fogarty School, Providence, NJ   Spring 2009
Social studies methods practicum
- Team planned and implemented a 5th grade social studies unit on New Jersey history using primary sources and children's historical fiction
- Planned an historical walking field trip with the NJ Historical Society

RELATED EXPERIENCE:

New Jersey College *Study Abroad Program*   January 2009
- Traveled to England for three weeks to learn about Great Britain's teacher education programs and national curriculum
- Observed and taught lessons in three different primary schools and attended classes at the University of Cumbria in Carlisle, England

Audubon Society of New Jersey, Bristol NJ   2006-2008
Teacher Assistant for ASNJ Environmental Education Program
- Planned and assisted director of education with school field trips to the Environmental Education Center and visits to school classrooms

RELATED SKILLS:

- Competent user of Microsoft Office (Word, Excel and PowerPoint), Front Page (web design), SMART Board, and novice user of classroom response systems and Tablet PC
- Fluent in Spanish

COMMUNITY VOLUNTEER

- Tutor, Inspiring Minds (Formerly VIPS)   Spring 2009
- Carpenter, Habitat for Humanity – New Orleans, LA   2008
- Fund-Raiser and Cyclist, NJ MS 150 Bike Tour   June 2007

EXTRACUR- RICULAR ACTIVITIES

- Treasurer, NJC's Future Elementary Teachers   2009-present
- Member, NJC's Student Chapter of NSTA   2008-present
- Interests: fitness, digital photography, travel

References Available Upon Request

Example of a Cover Letter

Albert Einstein
60 Genius Blvd., Princeton, NJ 08542
(609) 345-6789
aeinstein@njc.edu

May 17, 2010

Ms. Maria Santos, Director
Department of Human Resources
Providence Public Schools
97 Westminster Street
Providence, NJ 08765

Dear Ms. Santos,

I am pleased to apply for the elementary general education teacher position. I earned a BA in Physics and recently completed my M.AT. in Elementary Education at New Jersey College. I am well qualified for the position. I hold a New Jersey State Department of Education Elementary Grades 1-6 Professional Teacher Certificate and endorsement in special education. I have significant teaching experience with urban students. And, I am fluent in Spanish and proficient user of the SMART Board, Tablet PC, classroom response system, document camera, and pocket-sized camcorder.

I am well prepared to help Providence meet the challenge of raising the academic performance of all learners. Through six practicum experiences and a semester of student teaching, I bring skills and understanding of urban students and families, responsive classroom management, unit planning using a "backwards design approach," analyzing assessment data to improve student learning, and collaborating with colleagues and families.

One experience in particular deeply affected my thinking about ESL students. I mentored an 8-year old boy from a Chinese family. I learned about the home and school lives of children who straddle two cultures - a non-English speaking home culture and an American school culture. As a professional teacher, I play an important role in facilitating the "cultural shift" by differentiating instruction, building positive relationships with families (e.g., home visits, family math nights or publishing parties), and paving the road for students' success in post-secondary education and chosen careers.

I will be an asset to your school and district. I can identify with urban students' needs and interests. I have the ability to help any student and will not give up on my students. I will collaborate with my colleagues, school agencies, and families to solve problems and help all learners achieve high academic standards.

Thank you for considering my application. I look forward to an invitation to interview. You can contact me at (609) 345-6789 or email aeinstein@njc.edu.

Sincerely,

Albert Einstein
Albert Einstein

Develop a Hiring Portfolio

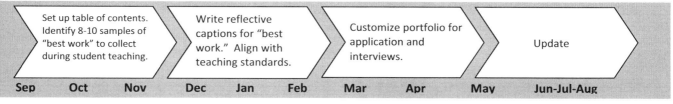

Sep Oct Nov	Dec Jan Feb	Mar Apr	May Jun-Jul-Aug
Set up table of contents. Identify 8-10 samples of "best work" to collect during student teaching.	Write reflective captions for "best work." Align with teaching standards.	Customize portfolio for application and interviews.	Update

A hiring portfolio demonstrates your ability to self-assess and think critically. A hiring portfolio is different from a credential file that contains job application materials. The portfolio can be a PDF file with hyperlinks, web-based, or a printed three-ring binder. The portfolio showcases evidence of your talents, education experience, and teaching abilities. A job applicant uses a hiring portfolio to present evidence while responding to questions. A hiring portfolio also represents an applicant's ability to organize, select evidence carefully and reflect upon the meaning of the evidence. Also, developing a hiring portfolio helps you mentally prepare for the job interview.

Tech-savvy job applicants use electronic portfolios. It's cheaper, easier to duplicate and mail with application materials. Portfolio development media used to create an e-portfolio include web-based pay-for-service (Chalk and Wire), free service (Google), Microsoft Office, or web design software (Publisher or Dreamweaver). Also, an e-portfolio can signal valuable technology experience. It can set you apart and give you "the edge." You can post an e-portfolio on the web. However, don't expect the interviewers to view it until you reach the final stage of hiring. You can bring an e-portfolio to an interview, but you will need to bring a laptop and digital projector.

Develop a printed and electronic portfolio with these components:
- Cover and statement of purpose
- Table of contents
- Cover letter and résumé
- Philosophy of education
- Images of teaching and learning
- Plan for a well-managed classroom
- Implemented unit and lesson plans, reflection
- Samples of student work at three different proficiency levels with commentary and rubrics
- Samples of professional development activity
- Parent communication

- Summary of results of an evaluation of your teaching by your students and supervisors
- Brief video clip of teaching and reflecting upon the lesson
- 3-5 reference letters

Include evidence of critical thinking by including an introductory reflective paragraph for each component. Relate your thinking to professional standards, theory and research about how students learn and effective teaching. Explain why you selected the item and what you learned. For images of you and students in the classroom, explain what you learned about the students or yourself from the teaching incident. Explain instructional decisions that helped your students learn. Or, explain how you would teach the lesson differently after reflecting.

Take a well-organized, printed portfolio (3-ring binder with sheet protectors and dividers) to the interview. Before you sit down for the interview, set your binder or laptop on the table. Open your hiring portfolio to an eye-catching component such as an action photograph of you teaching students. Do not hand the portfolio to the interviewer or place in your lap. Orient the portfolio so that the interviewers can view it easily. There may be one or two opportunities to use the portfolio during a 20-30 minute interview. Above all, don't "jump start" an interview with your portfolio and attempt to take control of the process. However, invite them to view your portfolio at the beginning.

Use the portfolio to illustrate points you would like to make while responding to interview questions. For instance, if you were asked *"How would you build a partnership with families?"* you could remove a brochure you created for "curriculum night" or a design of your class web page. Hand the brochure to the committee for further inspection while you explain several strategies for partnering with families.

Before you leave the interview, hand each interviewer a CD-ROM of your portfolio.

How to Use a Hiring Portfolio

Employers do not require job applicants to submit a hiring portfolio. It's common for job applicants to bring printed hiring portfolios to interviews. Some employers may recommend that job applicants do not bring or use portfolios during the interview because it distracts interviewers who need to listen, ask questions, and make judgments. Some interviewers prefer to view portfolios after the interview.

Some employers require applicants to submit additional evidence that demonstrates knowledge of teaching, critical thinking, and written communication. For instance, Providence Public Schools in Rhode Island require job applicants to submit essays about raising the achievement level of all of your students, using student performance data to drive instruction, and planning for professional development. Also, job applicants teach a 15-minute lesson to the interview committee and complete a proctored writing sample.

Regardless, developing a hiring portfolio will help you prepare for the interview by self-assessing your experience and achievements. You can compile a sample of "best work" that reflects your knowledge of teaching, skills, and experience and to demonstrate critical thinking. This time-consuming process prepares you mentally for the interview. It's a dress rehearsal. The by-product is a polished printed binder or an electronic document.

During the interview, make the interviewers aware of the portfolio. A skillful job applicant weaves relevant evidence from the portfolio into answers to interview questions. This takes practice. Know your portfolio well. Interviewers may browse the headlines but not the fine print.

There is nothing lost by presenting each interviewer a CD of a high quality e-portfolio at the end of an interview. This builds the interviewers' awareness of additional, available evidence. Some employers may review the portfolio if the job applicant moves to the final stages of the hiring process.

The hiring portfolio symbolizes your preparation and ability to organize, select evidence of "best work," and demonstrate critical thinking. If stored on a CD or on the web, your portfolio conveys "I am a teacher who uses technology."

Components of a Hiring Portfolio

Here are components of a hiring portfolio with suggestions of what to include.

Statement of Purpose

Write four or five sentences. The statement of purpose is the first item viewed by the reader. Treat it as a marketing tool. Sell yourself well. Briefly explain the purpose of the hiring portfolio and what the evidence demonstrates (e.g., "I am highly qualified for the specific position. I meet the specific criteria used for hiring." "I am a job applicant with unique knowledge, skills, and experiences." Highlight two or three personal strengths supported by the evidence within the portfolio.

Table of Contents
Here are a table of contents and suggestions for evidence and critical thinking for each component.
I.   Cover Letter
II.   Résumé
III.   Philosophy Statement
IV.   Images of Teaching and Learning
V.   Plan for a Well-Managed Classroom
VI.   Unit Planning with Two Implemented Plans
VII.   Reflection on Implemented Lesson
VIII.   Student Work – Assessment of Student Learning
IX.   Plan for Professional Development
X.   Results of an Evaluation of Teaching
XI.   Parent – Guardian Communication
X.   Other

I. Cover Letter
Insert a one-page cover letter. Customize the cover letter for the teaching position.

II. Résumé
Evidence: Insert a one to two page résumé. Customize the résumé for the teaching position.
Critical Thinking: Develop a reflective introductory paragraph for this section. Highlight several unique skills and experiences from the résumé that relate to the job qualifications, criteria for hiring, and mission of school or district. Identify several skills and experiences that distinguish you from other applicants. It is important that you stand apart from the many others who are applying for the same position.

III. Philosophy of Education
Evidence: Philosophy is defined as a set of beliefs and principles by which one lives. Knowing what you value or believe leads you to solutions to problems. Your future employers want to know if your philosophy of education relates well with the school or district mission and your future colleagues. *Are you a good fit??*

Developing a philosophy of education can be a soul-searching process that helps you communicate more effectively who you are as a teacher.

For this section of the portfolio, develop a two-page philosophy of education that responds to these prompts. *Why do I teach? What is my vision for teaching? What principles guide me as a teacher?* Below is a guide for writing a philosophy of education.

45

Paragraph 1: Explain several core beliefs about the purpose of education in the 21st century.

Paragraph 2: Explain your thinking about how students learn. Relate to theory, philosophy of education, and research/theory (e.g., psychology, cognitive science, biology) on how students learn, and guiding principles found in professional teaching standards.

Paragraph 3: Explain your beliefs about the roles of teachers and students in education. Explain preferred approaches to teaching and learning that help all students achieve high standards. Explain the design of the learning environment that supports students' learning in 21st Century classrooms.

Paragraph 4: Explain your vision for working collaboratively with others (e.g., colleagues, families, other community members) to plan and implement exemplary educational programs for all students.

Paragraph 5: Explain how you will develop your ability to teach as you move along the continuum from novice to expert.

Paragraph 6: Briefly explain why you are called to a career as a teacher. What's in it for you?

Other considerations: When you develop your philosophy of education, build upon an inspirational quote from a philosopher or notable educator that represents a core belief. Relate your beliefs to the mission of the school and district.

Critical Thinking: Develop a reflective introductory paragraph for this section. Relate to learning theorists and philosophers of education such as Mortimer Adler, Jerome Bruner, John Dewey, Reggio Emilia, Howard Gardner, Maria Montessori, Jean Piaget, Theodore Sizer, Socrates, and Lev Vygotsky.

IV. Images of Teaching and Learning

Evidence: Insert engaging images of your classroom instruction as well as related products of teaching and learning. The images with brief captions should tell a story and not merely be decorations. When inserting an image, ask yourself "Is this picture worth a 1000 words or even 100 words?"

Insert several images with different dimensions (25 % - 50 %- 100% of page) related to different aspects of teaching.
- *Instruction:* interactive functions of teaching, repertoire of models, methods and strategies, approach to teaching and learning, assessment and evaluation

- o *Organization:* building and maintaining a learning community, classroom management, materials management, long and short-term planning for instruction and assessment
- o *Leadership:* school leadership and collaboration with colleagues, parent-guardians, community agencies, unions and other professional associations

Critical Thinking: Develop brief reflective captions explaining the significance of the image. For instance, show an action photo of teaching a lesson and explain the instructional decisions used to support all learners. Explain what your learned as a result of teaching the lesson or what you would do differently if you taught the same lesson in the future. Relate your thinking to theory, research on best practices, professional teaching standards, or mission/expectations of the employer.

NOTE: For electronic portfolios, reduce resolution of images before inserting.

V. Plan for a Well-Managed Classroom
Evidence: Insert a two-page statement that outlines your classroom management plans. What principles of behavior management guide you? What strategies will you use? How will you organize and structure your classroom to help all students learn?
Critical Thinking: Develop a reflective introductory paragraph for this section. Relate your thinking to theory and research about behavior and classroom management, professional teaching standards, and well-established classroom (and school-wide) management programs.

VI. Unit Planning with Two implemented Lessons
Evidence: Insert a unit plan and two implemented lesson plans.
Critical Thinking: Develop a reflective introductory paragraph for this section. Explain the significance of unit and lesson planning as a function of teaching. Convey an understanding of the process of unit planning (e.g., *Understanding by Design* "backwards design approach"). Relate your thinking to theory, research on best practices, and professional teaching standards.

VII. Reflection on an Implemented Lesson
Evidence: Insert a reflection on one of the implemented lesson plans.
Critical Thinking: Develop a reflective introductory paragraph for this section. Explain the significance of reflection as an aspect of being a reflective practitioner and the iterative process of planning, teaching, and reflecting. Relate your thinking to theory, research on best practices, professional teaching standards, or mission/expectations of the employer.

VIII. Student Work – Assessment of Student Learning

Evidence: Insert three current samples of student work (one-two pages per sample) representing a range of student proficiency levels. Include the *task* that resulted in the student work, *procedures* for evaluating the work, *rubrics* for making judgments in relation to goals and standards, and r*ecording forms*. Indicate the *level of proficiency* of each work sample.

Critical Thinking: Write a commentary. Analyze the results of assessing the students' work. Explain the implications of reviewing student work and self-reflection on teaching and learning. Relate your thinking to theory, research on best practices, professional teaching standards, or mission/expectations of the employer.

NOTE: For electronic portfolios, insert scanned images. Reduce resolution of images before inserting.

IX. Plan for Professional Learning

Evidence: Insert a three-year plan for professional learning linked to professional teaching standards.

Critical Thinking: Develop a reflective introductory paragraph for this section. Explain the significance of planning for professional development. Relate your thinking to theory, research on best practices, professional teaching standards, or mission/expectations of the employer.

X. Results of an Evaluation of Teaching

Evidence: Insert an evaluation of your teaching from a supervisor (clinical instructor, cooperating teacher).

Critical Thinking: Explain the significance of reflecting on teacher evaluations. What are your strengths? What goals are you setting for future professional learning? Relate your thinking to theory, research on best practices, professional teaching standards, or mission/expectations of the employer.

XI. Parent – Family Communication

Evidence: Insert a parent-family communication such as a curriculum night brochure or letter to parents and families introducing a unit of study.

Critical Thinking: Explain the significance of communicating with parents and improving parent-teacher relationships. Relate your thinking to theory, research on best practices, professional teaching standards, or mission/expectations of the employer.

XII. Other

Video of Teaching

Evidence: Insert a three to five minute video clip of your teaching. Add footage of your personal commentary on your teaching. Or, insert the lesson plan with any handouts for a 15-20 minute lesson that you could teach to the interview committee.

Critical Thinking: Explain the significance of the video. Relate your thinking to theory, research on best practices, professional teaching standards, or mission/expectations of the employer.

Below are other components:

- *Certifications and licenses*
- *Evidence of honors and awards*
- *Score reports on required standardized tests for teaching*
- *Reports of criminal background checks by law enforcement personnel*
- *Letters of reference*
- *Individual education plan*
- *Materials that demonstrate an ability to differentiate instruction*
- *Lesson plan for a demonstration lesson*

Demonstrate Critical Thinking

Employers observe a job applicant's ability to think critically during an interview and required written essays, proctored writing samples, and hiring portfolios. To demonstrate critical thinking, introduce each section of your portfolio with a brief reflective paragraph (about four or five sentences). And, write reflective captions under digital images of teaching.

You can explain:

- reasons you selected the evidence for inclusion in the portfolio
- how the evidence relates to the school or district mission and job qualifications
- what you learned or achieved
- actions you will take to improve your teaching
- goals for future professional learning

When you write the paragraph or caption, relate your thinking to professional teaching standards and theory and research about how students learn and effective teaching.

Example of a Reflective Paragraph Introducing a Section

<u>Section: Unit Planning and Two Implemented Lessons</u>

In this section you can view evidence of my ability to plan a unit using a "backwards design approach." The unit planning framework centers on the idea that the design process should begin with identifying the desired results and then "work backwards" to develop instruction rather than the traditional approach of defining topics need to be covered. The framework includes three main stages:

Stage 1: Identify desired outcomes and results.

Stage 2: Determine what constitutes acceptable evidence of competency in the outcomes and results (assessment).

Stage 3: Plan instructional strategies and learning experiences that bring students to these competency levels.

Unit planning helps me focus on the big ideas, align with standards, and plan systematically for assessment of student learning.

(Professional Teaching Standard 2)

<u>Source</u>: McTighe, J. & Wiggins, G. (2005) *Understanding by design.* Alexandria, VA: Association for Supervision & Curriculum Development.

Example of Reflective Caption for an Image of Teaching and Learning

(Image of students using remotes)

Using Classroom Response Systems (CRS*) CRS engages all learners, increases student interaction, and improves critical thinking and assessment. I pre-assessed students during the FOSS* Earth Materials *science unit by using an emerging technology called classroom response system. I learned about my students' misconceptions and then planned lessons accordingly.*

(ISTE NETS Standard 2*: Design and Develop Digital-Age Learning Experiences and Assessments*)

Develop a Plan for Professional Learning

Develop a plan for professional learning that communicates to the interviewers the character trait of "constant learner." Often, the teacher certification office in a state department of education and/or your school district have a formal process of planning professional learning related to each teacher's area of certification. A plan can include these components: personal and professional goals, raising student achievement, improving teaching and learning, and school improvement initiatives.

You may not have a professional learning plan if you're graduating soon or recently completed your teaching education program. Below is a step-by-step procedure with an example:

Step 1: Reflect on areas to improve, formulate three or four goals and state a personal/professional rationale for each goal.

Step 2: Relate to professional teaching standards.

Step 3: Relate the goal to the type of professional learning activity.
- College or University Coursework
  Examples: Undergraduate and graduate level courses; M.Ed./CAGS/Ph.D./ Ed.D. Programs
- Workshop/Conferences/Training Sessions
  Examples: professional institutes/training sessions/audited courses/ workshops
- Collaborative and Partnership Activities
  Examples: applied studies with colleagues such as: mentoring, peer coaching, collegial study groups. Professional networks involve active participation in professional, education-focused organizations.
- Involvement in Development/Improvement Processes
  Examples: board, committee, school improvement team, advisory board development work, developing curricula, instructional units or assessments, parent/community outreach, school to work programs; school support with families/community
- Individually Guided Professional Learning
  Examples: independent study/educational project, educational travel, externship
- Professional Leadership Experiences
  Examples: national certification programs, publications and presentations

Step 4: Indicate the time period that you will engage in the professional learning activity and attain the goal.

A Plan for Professional Learning

Goal #	Goal with Rationale	Professional Teaching Standards	Type of Professional Learning Activity	Time Period
1	GOAL: I will increase my knowledge about how to develop unit plans using a "backwards design approach" and focus on "big ideas" in the curriculum. RATIONALE: To implement units with learning outcomes aligned to the district curriculum and Common Core Standards; a systematic plan for assessing student learning using a variety of assessments; and learning experiences using differentiated instruction and sequenced appropriately.	2, 3, 5, 8, 9	Graduate courses: ELED 513 *Designing and Assessing for Teaching and Learning*	2011-2012
2	GOAL: I will attain a Masters in Special Education with an emphasis in urban multicultural curriculum and instruction. RATIONALE: To learn how to accommodate diverse learners, develop IEPs, and work collaboratively to improve urban multicultural student performance in literacy, mathematics, and other subjects.	1, 2, 3, 4, 5, 6, 7, 8, 9, 10, 11	Graduate courses leading to a M.Ed. in Special Education	2010-2013
3	GOAL: I will learn about effective strategies that foster collaborative relationships with colleagues and families. RATIONALE: To support and improve students' learning and the classroom environment.	8	Team Participation	When hired by a school/ district
4	GOAL: I will increase my knowledge and skill of using instructional technology RATIONALE: To utilize available technologies for 21st Century classrooms, to engage learners and to improve instruction and assessment.	2, 3, 5, 8, 9	Training Sessions Smart Board Classroom Response Systems	2010-2011 2011-2012

Develop an Electronic Portfolio

Electronic portfolios can be as simple as a single file (PDF) with internal and external hyperlinks or a URL of a web-based e-portfolio. Job applicants inform employers about web-based e-portfolios by providing a URL on a résumé, cover letter, or thank you letter following an interview. When job applicants are interviewing, they can present the interview committee an e-portfolio stored on a CD or DVD.

e-Portfolio Development Media

Job applicants currently in teacher education programs use web-based pay-for-services such as Chalk and Wire and Live Text. Chalk and Wire, an assessment management system for colleges and universities, includes a feature for students to develop hiring portfolios. This service provides students different themes for backgrounds or they can customize. Students load and organize text, photos, video, audio, and other graphic images. Students easily update, copy, store, download to a computer and other storage devices, and share the portfolio with others by creating a URL. The cost is $49 for a one-year subscription or $84 for five years.

Interfolio.com is a service for storing and sending confidential documents to employers. The cost is $19 for a one-year subscription or $57 for five years. Documents may include (but are not limited to):

- Confidential and non-confidential letters of recommendation
- Résumé
- Statement(s) of purpose
- Writing samples
- Teaching portfolio documents
- Supervising teacher evaluations
- Student and peer evaluations
- Unofficial transcripts

You can use software such Microsoft Publisher, Adobe Dreamweaver, Microsoft Office, and Adobe Acrobat Pro to develop an online portfolio. Free services include Google Page Creator and Docs, Blogger and Word Press.

Types of Storage

Electronic portfolios can be stored on web and copied to a CD, DVD, or USB drive.

Work Offline and Proofread

Problems with grammar, spelling, or formatting will distract employers and leave them with a negative view of your ability to communicate. Develop the text offline using a word processing program. Proofread the text and examine the formatting before uploading to the web. Use these documents when printing a portfolio for an interview.

Designing an e-Portfolio

Designing an e-portfolio is a creative process requiring many decisions about colors, backgrounds, graphics and font types and sizes.

Use of Color

Light text colors on a light background are ineffective. Use contrasting colors for text and background. Tone down background colors or images so employers will focus on the text. Limit the number of different colors for text and the background. Select two or three complementary colors for your e-portfolio and use them consistently.

Font Types and Sizes

If the font is too large, the pages require too much scrolling. Popular web fonts are Verdana, Arial, Helvetica and Times Roman. Avoid fonts with prominent serifs or fancy, decorative fonts.

Graphic Images and Captions

Pictures, videos, scanned images and other visual material should not be too large in dimension and size. Too large images require too much scrolling. A too small image makes it difficult for the employer to view and interpret. If you use thumbnails, include an option to view a larger image in a separate window or page.

Reduce resolution or size of images from a digital camera before uploading. An original image can be 4 MB or larger. A small e-portfolio image (25% of a page) can be 50 KB and still have adequate resolution without distortion. Use software such as Windows Office Picture Manager, Apple iPhoto, or Google Picasa to reduce the size of your images.

Include captions for your graphic images. Explain what the image represents.

Attached Files

If including links to attached files (e.g., résumés, unit plans), format the document as a PDF before you upload to a web-based portfolio. Include a statement near the icon to direct the employer to click the icon or hyperlink to the attached file (e.g., "Click the icon to download the résumé.")

Testing Links

Test all internal and external links off- and on-line. View the e-portfolio on both Windows and Mac OS computers.

Develop a Printed Portfolio for an Interview

Bring a printed portfolio for your interview. Below is advice for developing a printed portfolio:

- Use a one-inch clear front vinyl binder.
- Use a color laser printer and high quality paper.
- Use plastic sheet protectors to help users turn pages easily and tab dividers to mark specific sections of the portfolio. Use both sides of a plastic sheet protector. Tab dividers should extend beyond the edge of the sheet protector.
- Create an engaging, eye-catching binder cover, table of contents, and labeled tabs for different sections.
- "A picture is worth a thousand words." It can be. Make sure yours does too. Devote two pages of the binder for an 11-inch x 17-inch display that tells an interesting story. Use PowerPoint to create slides with large photos and headings and sub-headings.
- Remove names on student work to insure anonymity and respect confidentiality.
- Include a CD of your e-portfolio in the printed portfolio.

Contact References

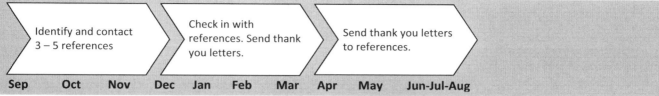

Typically, employers require applicants to list 3 - 5 references and include letters of recommendations with applications. During the screening phase, references are viewed briefly. If you're selected as a finalist, your letters of recommendation are reviewed more carefully and references may be called for further information.

The best references are experienced educators who have observed you teach recently.
If you're a recent graduate, ask your cooperating teacher and college supervisor to serve as a reference. Other pre-student teaching professors and clinical instructors can serve as references. Parents of students you've taught can serve as references, especially if they can write about how you positively influenced their students and actions you took to build partnerships between the school, classroom and home.

If you haven't completed your student teaching semester yet, invite your principal to observe you. Following the observation, schedule a meeting with the principal to reflect on the lesson. Prepare well for this meeting. This is a chance to promote yourself further and practice interviewing. Then, invite the principal to serve as a reference.

Other professional teachers you have worked with or supervisors from previous careers can serve as references. They can write about skills and personal qualities related to the job description.

Before listing the references in the job application, it is customary to ask your references if they would be willing serve as a reference.

If they agree, request their contact information during the academic year and the summer. Employers may contact the reference during the summer when they are not on the college campus or in school. Give your references adequate time to write the letter. Contact your references a month before you plan to submit your application. Inform them of a due date - when you need the reference so you can submit your application materials. If you haven't received the letter, politely remind them and explain that you would be glad to pick up the letter.

At the end of your résumé, type "References available upon request." If an employer requests contact information for references, you can attach a separate file to the résumé or enter into the section of the online application. Include the reference's title, first and last name, role, school, organization, or company, mailing address, phone, and email.

When you ask people to serve as a reference and/or write a letter of recommendation, send them your résumé and a job description.
Next, request an appointment to talk about the teaching position and your qualifications. When you meet in person or on the phone, talk enthusiastically about the teaching position and why you believe you're a good fit for the position. Draw attention to your unique skills, knowledge and experiences. Refer to your résumé. If you have a hiring portfolio, show them evidence of your abilities. This is also good practice for the job interview.

Send thank you letters to your references.

Example of a Request for a Letter of Recommendation

Albert Einstein
60 Genius Blvd., Princeton, NJ 08542
(609) 345-6789
aeinstein@njc.edu

May 17, 2010

Professor Barbara McClintock
Department of Elementary Education
New Jersey College
600 Mt. Pleasant Avenue
Providence, NJ 08765

Dear Professor McClintock,

Thank you so much for agreeing to serve as reference and to write a letter of recommendation for a classroom elementary teaching position in Providence Public Schools. Attached are my résumé and a job description. Your name is listed on the page following the résumé. I will also list your name in the online portfolio at SchoolSpring.com.

The application with your letter of reference is <u>due June 15</u>. To assist you in writing the letter, the Providence hiring committee will be assessing my knowledge and skills in five domains of effective teaching and five teacher competencies listed in the job descriptions

During student teaching, you evaluated my "Teacher Candidate Work Sample." I assessed grade 4 students in an urban classroom while teaching the hands on science unit called FOSS *Structures of Life.* I earned an A and was particularly proud of my performance and growing confidence in assessing students.

For the letter of recommendation, I hope you can refer specifically to my <u>ability to utilize assessment data to guide instruction and plan for the future</u>. This relates to the Domain of Effective Teaching #2 and #4. Also, in your evaluation you commented on my <u>ability to think critically and respond to the cultural and developmental needs of the students</u>. This relates to Teaching Competency #3.

Please address the letter to: Ms. Maria Santos, Director, Department of Human Resources, Providence School Department, 97 Westminster Street, Providence, NJ 08765. Enclosed is a stamped, addressed envelope.

Thank you for writing a letter of recommendation. If you have questions or concerns, you can contact me at (609) 345-6789 or email aeinstein@njc.edu.

Sincerely,

Albert Einstein
Albert Einstein

Example of a Thank You Letter to a Reference

Albert Einstein
60 Genius Blvd., Princeton, NJ 08542
(609) 345-6789
aeinstein@njc.edu

June 17, 2010

Professor Barbara McClintock
Horace Mann 209
Department of Elementary Education
New Jersey College
600 Mt. Pleasant Avenue
Providence, NJ 08765

Dear Professor McClintock,

Thank you so much for writing a letter of recommendation for the elementary classroom teaching position in Providence Public Schools. I really appreciate the time you took from your busy schedule to write this outstanding letter. I noticed how you included specific details about my abilities. This will help the hiring committee understand why I am the best person for the job!

I'm really excited about starting my career. I'm so grateful for your inspiration, your guidance during student teaching, and launching me on this life-long journey.

Have a great summer!

Sincerely,

Albert Einstein

Albert Einstein

Prepare for Interviews

| Sep | Oct | Nov | Dec | Jan | Feb | Mar | Apr | May | Jun-Jul-Aug |

Set up **"mock interviews"** with your cooperating teacher, college supervisor, and other veteran teachers. They can ask you typical interview questions and provide you feedback on your delivery and content of responses. Career counselors can assess your overall interviewing skills and suggest strategies to help you strengthen them.

Outline 3-5 points you want to make during the interview. Relate your strengths, skills, and accomplishments to the nature of the teaching position, mission of the school and district, and current issues such as federal and state mandates for improving student performance of all learners.

Outline and rehearse responses to typical interview questions. Make connections to the school/district curriculum, standards, and assessment system during the interview. Relate to research-based practices and key issues such as classroom management, differentiated instruction, collaborating with other teachers, and partnering with families. Also, be prepared to share a title of something that you have read recently, whether related to the profession or for pleasure.

If you're asked to *"describe a situation in which students you taught learned a significant lesson,"* explain how you used critical reflection to raise academic achievement of low-performing students or how you overcame barriers and worked collaboratively with other teachers and families to achieve high standards. Explain how you used feedback and resources to improve your teaching.

Examples of interview questions:
  a. *Why are you a good fit for this position?*
  b. *Tell us about your approach to teaching reading.*
  c. *Identify a performance standard and explain how you would teach this lesson to enable your students to achieve the standard.*
  d. *Describe a time when your authority was challenged or a class rule was broken.*
  e. *How would your students describe you?*

Remember: You're "interviewing" the school as well. Be prepared to ask questions about the school's initiatives and programs.

While speaking, be enthusiastic and passionate about teaching. Convey a belief that all students can learn and achieve at high levels, regardless of their backgrounds. Don't be afraid to pause for a few seconds after the question has been asked to gather your thoughts. Interviewers will recognize your intention to deliver an organized, thoughtful response.

First impressions are important. Dress for success. Groom well and dress neatly and conservatively. For men wear a two-piece matched suit and silk tie. For women, wear a two-piece matched pant or skirt suit. When you enter the room for the interview, smile, establish eye contact and shake hands with each member of the hiring committee.

When scheduling an interview for a position, ask the employer about the interview process. What are the names and positions of the interviewers? What is the physical setting? How long is the interview and how many questions are asked? Can you provide sample questions?

Arrive 30 minutes prior to the scheduled interview. Wait in your car and walk in five to ten minutes early.

Believe in yourself. Be yourself. Be courteous. Have a sense of humor. Learn from your mistakes. Keep moving forward.

Many final interviews include teaching a lesson to a committee or students in a classroom. Prepare an outstanding model lesson. Don't wing it.

Send thank you letters to your interviewers. Thank them for their time. Restate your interest in the job and enthusiasm for the teaching position, school and district. Write something that will help each interviewer remember you.

Common Interview Practices

There are several types of interviews. A <u>pre-screening interview</u> occurs at a teacher job fair with a recruiter. A <u>screening interview</u> is scheduled shortly after the application due date. A human resource department representative or screening committee member calls you for a 20-minute interview to determine if you meet the minimum qualifications.

Sometimes, the screening interview is over the phone, especially if you live beyond commuting distance of the district. You are not required to answer interview questions immediately upon answering the phone. It is unlikely that you will be ready to answer questions effectively on the spot. Instead, communicate your enthusiasm and ask when you might schedule the screening interview. When you speak on the phone during the interview, use a headset connected to your phone or use a speaker phone so you can take notes, sit next to your computer and view school or district information. If possible, use a land-line for better reception. Turn off call waiting or ignore incoming calls.

If you pass this screening interview, you are scheduled for a <u>second interview</u> that lasts about 60 minutes. A <u>third interview</u> may be scheduled for the top three finalists. Employers often require finalists to teach a model lesson to students or to an interview committee as part of the job hiring process. Following the lesson, you debrief the lesson with the committee. This is an opportunity for interviewers to observe your ability to reflect and think critically.

If possible, visit the school prior to your interview and observe a classroom, movement in the hallway between classes, and arrival and dismissal times. Knowing something about the school and the interview committee will help you relate to the interviewers and their questions. The interview committees may include administrators, teachers, parents, and community members. Learn the interviewers' names, titles, and positions before the scheduled interview.

Interviewers highly value etiquette such as arriving five to ten minutes early, professional attire, use of eye contact, confidence, warmth, and a sense of humor. (Don't confuse a sense of humor with telling jokes. This can be problematic.) You will enter a room with five to ten committee members who will probably be seated. It is customary for job applicants to introduce themselves and greet each interviewer with eye contact, a smile and a firm handshake. Eye contact is particularly important. Looking down or away does not display confidence.

The leader of the hiring committee begins the interview by introducing committee members and presenting background information on the position and the school (e.g., grade levels in the building, daily schedules, and unique building-wide instructional initiatives.).

Next, interviewers take turns asking questions. A common "warm-up" question is *Tell us about your background and what special skills you will bring to the position.* Develop a clear, succinct response to this question. This is your "60-second commercial."

Interviewers ask 7-10 questions that probe your knowledge, skills, and experiences with curriculum and instruction, raising achievement levels, using data to inform decision-making. *Tell us about your approach to teaching reading. How would you integrate content area reading while teaching science? What experience do you have raising achievement levels of your students?*

Interviewers ask a variety of questions to uncover dispositions toward self, students, and teaching. Strong interpersonal skills are critical to a job applicant's success. Interviewers pay attention to the content and depth of the responses, critical thinking, as well as the job applicant's verbal and nonverbal communication. They ask questions to get to know you personally such as *Describe your perfect day.* or *How do you create balance in your life?*

Sometimes, but not often, interviewers provide a list of interview questions to the job applicant *prior to the interview*. The job applicant is given a few minutes to read through the list. Then, the interview begins with the first question on the list. Or, they ask the job applicant to respond to the questions in any order.

Often, the interviewer concludes with the question, *What questions do you have for us?* Be prepared to ask questions that inform the interviewers that you have researched the school/district mission, initiatives, program, curriculum, and assessment (e.g., *How is the afterschool mathematics and science inquiry program working?)* Or, indicate an interest in continued professional learning (e.g., *Are there opportunities to learn how to use emerging technologies such as SMART Board and classroom response systems?*). Don't ask about the salary and benefits or if you can arrive a few days after the beginning of the school year because you need to attend a wedding!

Don't expect any feedback on your interview performance or application. Before you leave, ask when the hiring committee and superintendent will make a decision. And, thank them for the privilege of interviewing with this fine school district.

Typically, the superintendent and school board make a decision after receiving a recommendation from the hiring committee. The committee's judgment reflects the consensus of the committee and based on established criteria for judging job applicants.

Nonverbal and Verbal Communication

If you're feeling nervous, you're not alone. Most of us feel nervous during high-stakes interviews. But do everything possible to convey positive energy and confidence. You can feel more confident if you know something about the interview process and prepare well.

First impressions are made instantly. Be yourself, but be your "best self." Enter the room with a smile, greet each interviewer, offer a firm handshake, and look the person in the eyes long enough to notice their eye color. After brief introductions and light conversation, have a seat and get comfortable in your chair. You'll be sitting for 45-60 minutes.

Sit up straight and position yourself squarely in front of your interviewers. Place your hiring portfolio on the table and open it up to an attention-grabbing component such as an interesting, captioned photograph of you and your students. Orient the portfolio where others will notice it from their position.

What do you do with your hands and arms? Don't cross your arms over your chest or fidget with your fingers. Instead, fold your hands, place them in your lap, on your thighs or rest them comfortably on the chair armrests. Occasional hand gestures are acceptable. Also, make sure your hands and fingernails are clean and well manicured.

When answering questions, provide eye contact to different members of the committee and not only the person asking the question. Know your audience. If an interviewer asks a question about increasing parent involvement, make eye contact with the parent on the hiring committee. When an interviewer asks a classroom management question, look in the direction of the assistant principal in charge of discipline. He or she will be very interested in your response.

Speak clearly and precisely. Use an expressive voice. Vary your speed and tone of delivery. Use correct grammar, usage, and pronunciation. Use professional language but don't sound like a textbook. Use your personal experience as a way of providing examples. Be aware of jargon – especially if there are non-educator interviewers such as parents. If you use an acronym, explain what each letter means.

Stay on topic. Be succinct. Listen carefully and answer the question you are asked.

After an interviewer poses a question, it's acceptable to pause a moment and organize your ideas. Interviewers will recognize your attempt to deliver a more precise, organized answer. If you don't understand the question, ask the interviewers to repeat the question or ask them to clarify. This can buy you some time to organize your ideas.

Think of the response to a question as a mini-presentation with a beginning, middle, and an end. Apply the old saying for speeches, "Tell them what you're going to tell them (introduce the topic), tell them (provide details), and tell them what you told them (summarize the topic)." Using repetition helps the interviewers process your ideas and view you as an organized, logical thinker and speaker.

Use an organizing principle to relate ideas and cue the listener. For example,
- Interviewer: *What procedure do you use to handle discipline problems?*

Job Applicant: *I use a four-step procedure for handling discipline problems: First . . . Next . . . Then . . . Finally . . .*

- Interviewer: *What is your approach to teaching reading?*
  Job Applicant: *I've learned that there is no one single approach to teaching reading. When I teach reading, I use three instructional practices recommended by the* National Reading Panel. *The first practice is . . . The second practice is . . . and the third and final practice is . . .*

If you can't answer a question because you lack practical experience, be honest about the gap. Share your theoretical knowledge and explain that you are looking forward to gaining more practical experience. Tell the interviewers that developing knowledge in this area is one of your goals for professional development. Ask the interviewers about opportunities for mentoring and other forms of professional learning.

Communicating Dispositions

Employers want to know if you're good fit for the school and community. During the hiring process, they can determine:

- Do you relate well to students with diverse abilities and backgrounds?
- Can you relate well to the students' families and faculty?
- Are you flexible?
- Are you willing to consider different perspectives?
- Do you take initiative?
- Are you organized and timely?
- Are you empathic, thoughtful, and not impulsive?
- What do you love about teaching?

A job applicant's disposition is the most important selection factor in long-term success of a hired teacher (Wasicsko, 2006). Knowledge of your subject and teaching skills are important, but if you don't possess the right dispositions, you are considered a liability.

Employers ask a variety interview questions that uncover your dispositions towards self, students, and teaching:

Indicators of a Disposition Toward *Self*:
- Has an innate ability to identify with students with diverse abilities and backgrounds
- Has a positive yet realistic self-perceptions
- Exhibits a "can-do" attitude which is usually expressed by a belief he/she can help virtually any student

Indicators of a Disposition Toward *Students*:
- Thinks students are able, worthy and valuable
- Believes all students are capable of learning

Indicators of a Disposition Toward *Teaching*:
- Is people-oriented rather than thing-oriented
- Expends a good deal of effort building positive relationships with students, colleagues and the community
- Maintains a service orientation
- Recognizes the larger issues rather than the more immediate and less important ones and constantly asks themselves, "How will my students be better 10 years from now because of what we are doing today?"

Disposition Interview Questions

Below are examples of typical open-ended interview questions focusing on a job applicant's dispositions towards self, students, and teaching. Before the interview, outline your responses and rehearse the delivery with another person.

1. Why are you a good fit for this position at this time?
2. What is it about this position that interests you?
3. How would your students describe you?
4. Describe a time when your students learned a significant lesson.
5. What kinds of problems do people bring to you? What advice was given and what, if anything happened afterwards?
6. Describe a time when you had to deal with a difficult person.
7. If your life works out the best you can imagine, what will you be doing in five years?
8. Describe your perfect day.
9. How do you balance your life? What do you do for fun?
10. What questions do you have for us?

Responses to Disposition Interview Questions

Here are six "disposition" questions and possible responses of what to say, what not to say and other considerations.

1. *Why are you a good fit for this position at this time?*
   What to Say:
   - This is a common first interview question. This is your "sales pitch." Develop a well-organized two-minute response. Interviewers are looking for what you view as important and your understanding of the position, school, and district.
   - Convey enthusiasm for the position and working in the school and district.
   - Relate to job qualifications. Relate to challenges the school and district are facing. Explain how your knowledge and skills are needed.
   - Explain what distinguishes you from other candidates. For instance, if applying for an urban teaching position where Spanish is spoken by a majority of students, explain how you are fluent in Spanish and taught mostly in urban schools.

- Share one or two significant education experiences that developed your knowledge and skills required for the position.

What Not to Say:
- I recently graduated and am ready to teach.
- I meet the minimum qualifications.
- I was a student at this school and want to return to teach. Wouldn't that be awesome?!!
- I have subbed in this district.

2. *How do your students describe you?*
   What to Say:
   - Students think that I know them individually. They believe I am concerned about their individual learning needs and can relate to their diverse cultures, interests, and preferred modes of communicating.
   - Students recognize my efforts to individualize an assignment and accommodate their individuality. They experience engaging, dynamic units and lessons.
   - Students believe they have a voice in this classroom. They feel connected to each other and part of a learning community. They recognize my efforts to build positive relationships.
   - Students understand that I am passionate about learning. I am a good role model as a reader, writer, and thinker.
   - Students respond to my high, achievable standards and clear expectations. The classroom is well managed, yet there is room for spontaneity. I use the teachable moment.
   - Other considerations: Focus on your strengths, but be prepared to answer the next question: *What are your weaknesses?* Focus on your ability to create a learning environment that supports all learners. Use your hiring portfolio and show examples of student evaluations of your teaching.

   What Not to Say:
   - I am a fun teacher.
   - I am totally spontaneous. Anything goes in my classroom!

3. *What are your weaknesses?*
   What to Say:
   - There is always room for improvement. I am growing as a teacher along of a continuum of novice to expert teaching. I self-assess, set goals for professional learning, and take specific actions.
   - One of my weaknesses is a common challenge faced by teachers.
     NOTE: Some common challenges (with solutions) include:
     - managing time for instruction (Allocate use of time carefully. Use a kitchen timer to pace the students and teacher.)

- o differentiating instruction for a wide range of learners (Work collaboratively with special education teachers.)
- o integrating subject areas (Understand the relationship of performance standards across different content areas. Apply the *Understanding by Design* approach in unit planning.)
- o keeping up to date with innovations in instructional technology (Set annual professional goals for learning a new instructional technology. Add to repertoire of practices.)
- Use "Problem-Action-Result" approach. First, state the challenge you're facing. Next, explain how you became aware of the weakness through continuous assessment of student learning and self-evaluation. Then, explain the specific actions you are taking action to improve. Finally, explain what you have learned from taking action.
- Other considerations: Be honest. Demonstrate you are a teacher who improves through self-reflection. Tell the interviewers that you hope to get a mentor who provides feedback on your teaching.

What Not to Say:
- Avoid revealing weaknesses that may be perceived as character flaws (e.g., "I'm a little disorganized and have trouble getting to places on time." "I'm a shy person and not a very good public speaker.")
- Don't reveal weaknesses related to classroom management, handling discipline problems, working with unruly students or difficult parents, or teaching core subject areas.

4. *What questions do you have for us?*
   What to Say:
   - Examples include:
     - o How is your new school-wide behavior management system (e.g., Positive Behavior Interventions and Supports) working? Has the school detention rate diminished or attendance rate increased? I had experience with PBIS during my student teaching semester.
     - o What types of support systems can I expect as a new teacher to the school? Does the school or district provide an orientation and mentoring program?
     - o What types of instructional technology are available to teachers and students?
     - o I read on your website that you received funding for SMART Boards and classroom response systems. How will teachers be supported with professional development? I have some experience with both technologies. One of my goals is to develop and share with colleagues a bank of SMART Board lessons and use classroom response systems for formative assessment during instruction.
     - o What achievements at the school are a source of pride to you and school community? What is your most significant accomplishment as a school or district during the past three-five years?

- o How would you describe the culture of your school?
- o I read on your web site that raising the achievement levels of all learners is part of your mission. Teachers and administrators are using assessment data for decision-making. How is this strategy working?
- Other considerations: This is a typical, final interview question. To improve your response, research the school and district before the interview. Interviewers will notice your curiosity or interest in particular school/district initiatives and whether you can relate your knowledge, skills, and experience to a specific school initiative. Be prepared to engage in discussion.

What Not to Say:
- What is the salary for first year teachers? How many personal days do we get?
- Will it be a problem if I miss the first two days of the school year? My best friend is getting married on Labor Day weekend.
- No. You've answered all my questions.

5. *How do you balance your life? What do you do for fun?*
   What to Say:
   - Begin by explaining that teaching can be stressful and that balance is critical to meet the everyday demands on your energy. Maintaining physical and mental health is critical. And, explain that effective teachers are active learners, always building knowledge and experience related to professional and personal interests.
   - Here is an example of something I've been learning related to a personal interest... (something not required as part of your teacher education program or professional development.)
   - I make sure I reserve time for …. (e.g., maintaining physical fitness, playing sports, traveling, volunteering, reading, learning to play a musical instrument or other hobby, home improvement, exploring nature, going to museums, spending time with friends and/or family).
   - Other considerations: "Being a teacher is more than a job and less than a life." (Wasicsko, 2006). Explain three or four things you do to balance your life. Convey positive energy and motivation to learn. Help your interviewers understand that you are people-oriented, and excited about life and all of its possibilities – inside and outside of school.

   What Not to Say:
   - I don't have much time for much more than teaching and my second job.
   - I need my alone time. I unwind with a glass of wine at the end of the day. And, I watch a movie or my favorite TV show. (Alone time for activities such as yoga or Tai Chi is considered a good thing, but don't stop there in your response.)
   - I go out to clubs with my friends.

6. *Describe a time when you had to deal with a difficult person.*
   What to Say:
   - Describe a personal experience you had with a student or a parent that ended with a positive result.
   - Organize your response using "PAR" (problem, action, results).
   - Building and maintaining positive relationships is key to effective learning. Explain the actions you took to maintain dignity, respect, and trust.
   - Explain what you learned from the experience and how it helped you improve your interpersonal skills.
   - Other considerations: It's acceptable to mention that you met in confidence with other knowledgeable people (e.g., guidance counselor, social worker, school psychologist) about the difficult person to gain some insights and talk through your strategy for solving the problem. When responding to the question, maintain confidentiality. Don't reveal the names of individuals.

   What Not to Say:
   - I've never had that problem. (Nobody will believe you!)
   - I'm an easy-going person. Most people get along with me. (That may be true, but this doesn't answer the question.)
   - Don't describe a situation with a personal friend, significant other, or family member.

Communicating Knowledge of Teaching and Critical Thinking

Interviewers pose different types of questions to determine knowledge of teaching, critical thinking, personal responsibility, commitment, constant learning, and communication skills. Often, interviewers learn about your personal qualities related to effective teaching by presenting a situation or problem that requires you to use knowledge about teaching and learning, to think logically, creatively and critically, and to communicate effectively. You need to deliver succinct, well-organized, and logical responses.

Relate Theory to Practice
When responding to these interview questions, relate personal experiences to theory, philosophy of education, educational research, and standards for effective teaching. Make connections to the school/district curriculum, national and state standards, and assessment systems.

Organizing Framework
You may be asked to respond to questions about a specific teaching situation, problem or challenge. One way to deliver your response to these types of questions is to use an organizing framework called Problem-Action-Result (PAR) (Clement (2006). When responding, begin by building a context and clearly stating the problem or challenge. Next, explain the actions you took to solve the problem. Then, explain the results of taking action and propose possible future

actions. Here is an example of a "PAR" response to the question, *How have you integrated technology into your teaching?*

Problem:
Early in my teacher education program, I learned in instructional technology course about the SMART Board as effective, interactive learning tool for teaching. During my student teaching semester, I discovered an unused SMART Board in the school hallway. I decided to use the technology to enhance student learning of Grade 4 geometry. The problem was I had no clue how to use it effectively.

Action:
I asked the school's computer teacher to teach me how to use the hardware and software and arrange the classroom furniture so everyone could view it. I prepared several SMART Board files and planned to involve small groups of students at the board at different points during the lessons.

Result:
Admittedly, it was a little awkward in the beginning. But I discovered that all my students were highly engaged, particularly many low-functioning special needs students. The principal was so impressed that she invited me to demonstrate the use of the SMART Board at a faculty meeting. This experience increased my confidence and desire to use other technologies. My next goal is to learn how to use classroom response systems to assess students' prior knowledge at the beginning of units.

Common Knowledge of Teaching Interview Questions
Below are examples of typical open-ended interview questions focusing on a job applicant's knowledge of teaching and critical reflection. Before the interview, outline your responses and rehearse the delivery with another person.

Working with Diverse Learners
- How have you modified assignments for English language learners (ELL)?
- Tell me about a student you have worked who had learning challenges. How did you structure lessons to meet these needs?
- What kinds of stresses do today's students face and how have you helped them cope with their concerns?
- How have you met the needs of high-functioning (e.g., gifted, talented) students in your classes?
- How have you helped low-functioning special needs students achieve academic success in your classes?

Curriculum and Standards
- Identify a state performance standard and explain how you have taught a lesson addressing that standard.
- Your students are not achieving the mathematics performance standard related to problem-solving. How would you close the gap in their achievement?
- How have you supplemented the hands on science module in your class?
- What is your approach to teaching literacy (mathematics, science, social studies)?
- How do you plan a unit?

Instruction
- If I walked into your classroom at 9 AM, what would it look like? What would you be doing?
- Describe how you would teach a lesson for a one-hour time period.
- Which teaching methods or approaches to learning do you employ most frequently?
- Describe any project or group work that has been successful with students.
- How have you integrated technology in your teaching?
- One of the goals for Grade 1 mathematics is *Students begin to add and learn their addition facts.* Explain how you could help them know and understand addition facts.

Assessment and Evaluation
- Explain how you assess student learning during a unit of instruction.
- Explain your expectations for evaluating a performance on a particular assignment as though you were explaining it to your class.
- How do you know a student understands a concept? What do you look for?
- Give an example of an assessment that changed your teaching or students' learning.
- What can you do as a teacher to narrow the achievement gap?
- How have you prepared students for standardized tests?

Classroom Management
- Explain your classroom management plans to me as though you were explaining it to your students.
- Describe a time when your authority was challenged or a class rule was broken and how you reacted.
- What have you done in the past to refocus a class and get it back on task?

Communication with Families
- How do you communicate long-range plans to students, parents, teachers, and principal?
- How would you communicate with parents that their child should be tested for special education services?

Professionalism
- How have you stayed current in your subject matter and in the field of teaching?
- How do you feel about the state, district or school's use of standardized test performance of students in evaluating your performance as a teacher?

Possible Responses to Knowledge of Teaching Interview Questions

Here are 23 "knowledge of teaching" questions and possible responses of what to say, what not to say and other considerations.

<u>Working with Diverse Learners</u>

1. *How have you modified an assignment for English-language learners (ELL) or special education students in your class?*

   What to Say:
   - Modify the assignment according to World-Class Instructional Design (WIDA) proficiency levels of your ELL students (e.g., Entering, Beginning, Developing, Expanding, Bridging).
   - Provide scaffolding so that ELL students can participate.
   - Select developmentally appropriate materials and activities for them.
   - Use careful grouping practices to make sure they are well supported.
   - Collaborate with the ELL teacher to learn of their needs and how to work together to support them.
   - Teach literacy skills with an understanding that ELL are second language learners. Therefore, it's important to concentrate on reading comprehension and vocabulary development over phonics in a language they are still learning.
   - Use both state standards and WIDA standards when planning lessons.

   What Not to Say:
   - Speak more slowly.
   - Provide ELL students extra time.
   - Let ELL students work with someone who speaks their native language. (Note: It is great to give ELL students native language support. However, ELL students also need plenty of access to English, their new language. In general the teacher should be delivering comprehensible instruction and not relying on translation by other students in the class as the primary way to provide instruction.)
   - Refer the ELL student to ELL teacher. "Doesn't the ELL teacher work with those students?"
   - I don't know. I have never worked with ELL students, but I would try my best to teach them.

2. *How have you met the needs of high-functioning students (e.g., gifted, talented) in your classes?*

   What to Say:
   - Tap into their unique interests, talents and creativity.
   - Use Revised Bloom's Taxonomy to plan lessons with learning outcomes and activities that cause learners to apply higher-level thinking.

- Use project-based learning in different curriculum and subject areas that cause learners to solve problems, engage in inquiry, synthesize factual and conceptual knowledge and communicate their understanding in different ways.
- Have students work with different types of students (e.g., other students who are gifted, students who are not functioning as high as them, and general education students). Help build their leadership skills in small groups and learn from their peers.

What Not to Say:
- Since they are so bright they will be fine. I can focus on my kids who really need my help.

3. *What kinds of stresses do today's students face and how have you helped them cope with stress?*
   What to Say:
   - Stresses include out of school factors (e.g., poverty, poor nutrition, lack of supervision due to absent parents, families moving from school to school, lack of support for homework, a different home culture than the mainstream school culture, substance abuse, domestic violence) and in school factors (e.g., academic pressure to achieve higher standards, peer pressure, bullying and teasing).
   - Strategies for helping students cope include: Know your students. Build a safe classroom community based on trust, mutual respect and openness. Be flexible. Respond to students' needs. Differentiate instruction. Know the resources in the school that are available to students and teachers. Engage families in your students' education (e.g., communicate plans for learning with families, provide the parents a "pledge for success" to sign as a way to build awareness of your expectations of their role in the students' education).
   - Other considerations: Explain that you will build relationships with school professionals (e.g., guidance counselor, social worker, school psychologist) and continue to develop your knowledge of issues facing students and appropriate actions to take in the classroom.

   What Not to Say:
   - Students need moral and character development.
   - Students aren't like they were when I was growing up. How can we ever raise their achievement levels?

4. *How have you helped low-functioning, special needs students achieve academic success in your classes?*
   What to Say:
   - Differentiate instruction based on the students' specific strengths and needs.
   - Use "pyramid planning," a framework for planning learning outcomes in different content areas.
   - Use "evidence-based" practices. Be prepared to say which ones!

- Use peer mentoring.
- Showcase students' successes. Create an atmosphere of pride and support no matter how small the learning step.
- Other considerations: Provide an example that relates to specific types of individual disabilities.

What Not to Say:
- I create lower expectations for students. They can't achieve the same levels of proficiency as other students.
- I teach all my students the same way with the same curriculum.
- I don't work with special needs students. The special education teacher works with them.

5. *Tell me about a student you have worked who had "learning challenges." How did you structure or modify lessons to meet these needs?*
   What to Say:
   - Follow the school's problem-solving and Response to Intervention process.
   - Use data to decide on various interventions. Monitor the students' progress frequently and change teaching actions based on the data.
   - Modify according to the student's strengths and needs.

   What Not to Say:
   - The student does not get any special help.
   - I expect the student to learn as his/her peers do. I don't want to baby the student.

Curriculum and Standards

1. *How do you increase your students' reading fluency?*
   What to Say:
   - Have students identify the purpose for reading before they begin to read.
   - Provide students with opportunities to read silently before attempting to read the material aloud in front of others.
   - Allow a second reading of the material. This will also increase their comprehension.
   - Provide reading material at the students' independent or instructional level.
   - Provide interesting reading material that is relevant to the students' lives and interests.
   - Help students increase sight vocabulary.
   - Use sound instructional practices such as "Reader's Theater."
   - Teach students the necessary critical punctuation and how it affects fluency.
   - Other considerations: Explain that fluency is one of the "five pillars" that the National Reading Panel identified with excellent reading. Although, fluency correlates with reading comprehension, fluency does not lead directly to comprehension.

What Not to Say:
- Just let students read.

2. *Explain your approach to teaching literacy.*
   What to Say:
   - Effective teachers of literacy are readers and writers. Students need good models of readers and writers. Teachers should read/write extensively and share reading/writing with their students. Teachers should demonstrate how reading and writing provide richness in their lives.
   - Provide students access to interesting and varied reading materials.
   - Provide opportunities for students to discuss their reading and writing with their peers.
   - Developing oral language leads to the development of reading.
   - Introduce students to as many words as possible in context.
   - Develop students' background of experiences. Activate background knowledge before beginning to read.
   - Set clear purposes for reading and writing.
   - Write the words encountered in reading.
   - Focus attention on getting meaning and in encoding meaning.
   - Other considerations: Refer to the National Reading Panel and National Writing Project. Know the school/district beliefs about how students learn to read/write and their reading/writing programs. Convey your beliefs about how students learn to read. Be prepared to respond to a follow-up question: *Tell us about your personal reading and writing.* Share a book you're read for pleasure and the most recent professional book or article. Inform the interviewers that you are member of the International Reading Association and/or National Council of Teachers of English.

   What Not to Say:
   - I can't think of a title of a book I'm reading at the moment.
   - There is only one way to teach reading.

3. *Explain your approach to teaching science.*
   What to Say:
   - Relate science concepts and skills to students' lives.
   - Motivate students by using interesting materials and science phenomena.
   - Students develop science concepts and skills by using a hands-on, multi-sensory approach to learning.
   - Inquiry is the preferred model of teaching. Learning of science requires students to apply thinking and processes of scientists.
   - Students can learn science by observing digital photographs and videos, and reading materials. These approaches can enhance learning following a hands on experience. Use

available instructional technologies to enhance science learning such as online simulations, digital microscopes, and SMART Board.

- Use effective questioning and responding to students' ideas (wait time).
- Direct instruction is used to teach science procedural knowledge such as how to use a microscope or how to conduct a procedure for an experiment.
- Integrate the teaching of science to teaching of writing. Use scientist notebooks to improve students' scientific thinking and communication.
- Relate scientific thinking skills to literacy, mathematical, social studies thinking skills.
- Provide students guided practice with problem-solving and inquiry test items. Develop students' metacognitive strategies. Use writing and thinking prompts related to sample test items.
- Other considerations: Relate to philosopher John Dewey. Refer to National Science Education Standards and *Reading Standards for Literacy in Science and Technical Subjects 6–12* Common Core Standards. Know the state performance standards and school/district science programs.)

What Not to Say:
- There is only one way to teach science.
- Teach science as a reading activity. Students need to develop vocabulary.

4. *Your students are not meeting a specific performance standard. How would you close the gap in their actual and desired academic achievement?*
   What to Say:
   - Convey your beliefs about how students learn. All students can learn if we provide them with the supports.
   - Relate a personal effort to close the gap using a personal experience. Explain the situation and relevant contextual factors (e.g., nature of individual learners, classroom instruction, and school/community).
   - Consider needs of individual learners (e.g., cognitive, physical, and emotional development, culture, personality, temperament). Focus on developmental and cultural needs of individual learners. Scaffold their learning. Provide coaching during independent work time during the school day and after-school tutoring.
   - Consider approaches that focus on social learning. Assign learners to small groups to maximize their learning. Use peer learning and cooperative structures such as jigsaw where students teach and learn from each other.

What Not to Say:
- Some students simply can't learn because of their home environments. What they need most is a lot of love and support.

5. *Your students are not achieving the mathematics performance standards related to problem-solving. How would you close the gap in their actual and desired academic achievement?*
   What to Say:
   - Provide students many opportunities to solve problems through use of manipulatives. Students generally learn better through their actions and interactions (with each other and with manipulatives)
   - Learning to problem-solve isn't only about learning the process. Since students aren't meeting the standards, make sure they are communicating their thinking to each other. If they share their approaches, students can learn from each other and I can acknowledge the strategies they use.
   - Instead of telling them what strategies to use, have students tell other students or me their strategies. While listening to the explanations of their strategies, help them make connections to the mathematics and to the strategies used.
   - In subsequent classes I would continue to help them make connections and ways they used similar strategies in other situations.
   - Other considerations: Focus your response on specific actions you can take in the classroom. Avoid talking about external contextual factors (e.g., substandard instructional materials, lack of parental involvement at home) for the problem of low achievement. Explain the term "manipulatives" to interviewers who are not educators.

   What Not to Say:
   - I don't like the math series we use. It doesn't teach them about problem-solving.
   - They are not doing their homework and it is really hard when I can't get help from home.

Instruction

1. *If I walked into your elementary classroom when students arrive, what would it look like? What would you and your students be doing for the first 15-20 minutes?*
   What to Say:
   - You notice a calm classroom. Students know the expectations and routines. I am greeting students when they walk in the door.
   - Making efficient use of time is critical since instructional time is limited. When students arrive at 9 AM, I have well-developed routines in place to begin the day.
   - Students know how to arrive and prepare to learn while class members and I take care of business (e.g., attendance, lunch count, work with a student who was absent the previous day). Students know the daily morning routine: Walk in quietly, say hello, store backpack and coats, read the posted agenda, submit homework, sharpen pencils, assume any class jobs, and work on the "Problem of the Day."

- I transition to the first lesson using a community-building activity such as the class song and pledge. Periodically, we sit together on the rug and have a class meeting. Then I begin the lesson.
- I am prepared to greet the students. Before I depart the previous day, I create the SMART Board file "Problem of the Day" and schedule, rotated the class jobs, update the lesson planning book, and prepare materials for the hands on science lesson.

What Not to Say:
- I'm not a morning person. It takes me a while to get my engines going. I give students some free time while I drink a cup of coffee and check the box scores and email on my iPhone.

2. *How do you insure that cooperative small group work is successful with your students?*
What to Say:
- I use flexible grouping strategies. I plan small group work according to the instructional goal, activity, and student learning needs. Sometimes students self-select the groups. Other times I assign students to groups according to their diverse learning needs.
- Start the year with groups of two and then move to groups of four after they develop the social skills needed for larger groups.
- Arrange furniture so students can face each other.
- Assign each group member a task and role to engage them simultaneously. Explain roles before they begin the activity. Rotate the roles.
- Develop a "quiet signal" for smooth transitions from small group to whole class.
- Use cooperative structures such as think-pair-share, jigsaw, numbered heads together.
- Create assignments or assessments to insure individual accountability for learning.
- Develop interpersonal skills needed for cooperative group work.
- Use class meeting time to solve problems and develop leadership skills. Help students understand what it means to work collaboratively. Have students self-assess their social behaviors.
- Monitor small group work. After setting students for small group work, move around the room and facilitate.
- Devote some instructional time to team-building activities (e.g., develop group name, logo, banner)
- Other considerations: Refer to a component of your hiring portfolio focusing on plans for a well-managed classroom or an implemented lesson that included cooperative group work.

What Not to Say:
- I've never had a successful experience with cooperative small group work.
- Students don't have the social skills. It takes too much time away from instruction to solve interpersonal conflicts that comes from small group work.

3. *Describe how you would teach a one-hour lesson.*
    What to Say:
    - Use your personal experience. Build the context for the lesson. Explain how the lesson is part of a well-sequenced series of lessons from a unit and aligned to specific district curriculum, state performance standards, and instructional materials.
    - Explain the learning outcomes for the lesson and the plan for informal assessment.
    - Explain how you planned for materials, time, and space.
    - Explain that planned learning experiences should be engaging and include opportunities for scaffolding.
    - Begin the lesson with a brief discussion that helps students link to prior learning (lesson or homework). Clarify goals and share the "agenda." Engage students by establishing set or background knowledge. End the lesson with a closure to help students summarize their learning. Link to future learning.
    - Other considerations: Refer to an implemented lesson plan in your hiring portfolio. Explain how you differentiated instruction for students with diverse learning needs. Include the use of technology to enhance learning. Explain what you learned as a teacher from teaching this lesson and how you would modify it in the future. Explain the reasons for different components such as scaffolding, establishing set, and closure. Identify the planned model(s) of teaching (e.g., inquiry, problem-based learning, direct instruction, presentation) or approaches (e.g., process writing, guided reading, cooperative learning, learning cycle) that help you achieve the learning outcomes.

    What Not to Say:
    - Describe a fun activity from beginning to end without explaining how you planned it or what you learned as a teacher from teaching the lesson.

Assessment and Evaluation

1. *Explain how you assess student learning during a unit of instruction.*
    What to Say:
    - Planning for assessment begins by making decisions about the end result (i.e., what students should know and be able to do) and then work backwards to plan assessment and planned learning experiences.
    - Use different types of assessments with different purposes: diagnostic, formative, and summative assessment.
    - Assessment provides feedback about what is working and what needs improvement about teaching and learning; helps to track student development of concepts and skills; and provides students with opportunities to monitor their learning and set personal goals.
    - Use a variety of types of assessments to assess different types of knowledge, ways of thinking, and attitudes and to accommodate learning preferences of students.
    - Other considerations: Present a brief, clear definition of assessment. Refer to the

backwards design approach to planning units (Jay McTighe and Grant Wiggins' *Understanding by Design)*. Provide an example in your hiring portfolio of how using the results of an assessment changed how you taught a concept or skill.

What Not to Say:
- Use assessments to grade students.
- Give students quizzes and end of unit multiple-choice tests.

2. *Explain your expectations for evaluating a performance on a particular assignment to me as though you were explaining it to your class.*
   What to Say:
   - The key to improving students' learning and achieving standards is providing clear expectations for a performance.
   - Use rubrics and checklists.
   - Provide a model of the performance. Ask students to use the rubric to assess the model.
   - When introducing the assignment, ask students to suggest criteria or develop a rubric for a performance.
   - Other considerations: Use your hiring portfolio. Use an example of a rubric or criteria checklist with student work at different levels of proficiency.

   What Not to Say:
   - Students want to know how to earn an A grade.
   - This is the score you need to earn an A, B, C, D and F.

3. *How do you know if your students understand a concept? What do you look for?*
   What to Say:
   - Use a rubric to assess and communicate clear expectations of what it means to "understand the concept" (e.g., definition, critical attributes, examples, nonexamples, relationship to other related concepts) to my students.
   - Use informal assessments (e.g., observation of students' responding to questions during a K-W-L discussion or classroom Jeopardy, journals, student activity sheets created during instruction) to assess factual knowledge related to the concept.
   - Use different types of formal assessments. To assess students' understanding of factual knowledge related to the concept, consider selected response items such as multiple choice, T/F, or matching. To assess conceptual knowledge requiring higher level thinking, consider academic prompts (brief constructed responses) or performance assessments. A Venn diagram or a "Same-Different T" chart would be useful for assessing students' ability to compare and contrast two related concepts. An example of a performance assessment is assessing a student who teaches a mini-lesson to other students.

- Consider students' preferred modes of communicating (e.g., writing, drawing, speaking, performing, using PowerPoint or a Podcast) to accommodate a wide range of learning needs.
- Provide students a pre-assessment to establish a baseline for knowing how their thinking improves as result of instruction or to help me know their misconceptions before I begin to teach the concept.
- Ask students to self-assess.
- Other considerations: Define the term "concept" at the beginning of your response. Use an example of assessing a concept from personal experience. Refer to your implemented lesson in your hiring portfolio as an example. Explain how you would use Revised Bloom's Taxonomy to develop questions or activities to assess student understanding.

What Not to Say:
- Say, "Raise your hand if you understand the concept." If most hands are raised, then I'm satisfied that they understand.
- Sample the class at the end of the lesson and ask a few comprehension questions. If several students answer correctly, I can safely assume the rest of the class understands and move on.
- If 80% of the class understands the concept when I quiz them, then I know a majority understand. That's good enough. I need to move on and cover the curriculum.

4. *Give an example of an assessment that you used to improve your teaching or students learning.*
What to Say:
- Use the component in your hiring portfolio containing three samples of student work at different levels of proficiency, the assessment task, and rubric.
- Explain how you planned and implemented the assessment, analyzed the results, and self-evaluated by using the assessment data to make decisions about improving teaching and learning.

What Not to Say:
- Assessment is my weakest area.
- I returned the graded exam with the answer sheet. This improved their understanding of the material. I could see by the results that they needed to study more.

5. *Identify a state performance standard and how you have taught a lesson addressing that standard.*
What to Say:
- Use the "backwards design approach" to planning the lesson and align it with the planned unit of instruction.

- State the standard and learning outcome and relate an informal assessment and planned learning experience. Describe an informal assessment and an accommodation for a student with special needs.
- Relate the lesson to a planned unit of instruction so that it's not a stand-alone lesson.
- Other considerations: Use your hiring portfolio. Select an implemented lesson plan which includes the standard.

What Not to Say:
- Explain a fun activity without relating the activity to a standard, learning outcome, or informal assessment.

6. *How do you prepare students for standardized tests?*
   What to Say:
   - Integrate essential concepts and skills from state performance standards into dynamic, engaging units and lessons.
   - Develop comfort and confidence with different question formats. Model the types of questions used in the tests. Integrate them into units and lessons.
   - For math and science, provide students guided practice with problem-solving and inquiry test items during instruction. Develop students' metacognitive strategies. Use writing and thinking prompts related to sample test items.
   - Other considerations: Demonstrate understanding of relevant district and state standardized tests and performance standards. Provide an example of how to improve their performance in an area where the school/district is low-performing.

   What Not to Say:
   - I drill and kill the entire year. A major part of my teacher evaluation relies on raising student achievement on standardized tests. I don't want to lose my job!

Classroom Management

1. *Explain your classroom management plan to me as though you were explaining it to your students and their parents/guardians.*
   What to Say:
   - I begin the school year by developing with my students a list of expectations for successful learning. This would turn into a brief "class pledge" with a list of five important expectations. Students sign the pledge and agree to follow these expectations.
   - Explain the system of providing consequences for on-task and off-task behaviors.
   - To make things run smoothly, we practice every day routines with students (pencil sharpening, using bathrooms). We have regular class meetings to analyze problems, discuss what's working and what needs to improve.

- Other considerations: Begin with a brief one or two sentence definition of classroom management. Outline the plan in five sentences and then ask the interviewers if they would like more details. Relate your classroom management system to the school-wide management system such as Positive Behavior Interventions and Supports. Refer to well-known programs or approaches to classroom management you know such as the Northeast Foundation for Children's The Responsive Classroom, Canter Assertive Discipline, and Glasser Approach.

What Not to Say:
- I don't really have a plan. I never have problems with students.
- I haven't really thought about it much since I recently graduated and never had my own classroom.

2. *Describe a time when your authority as an elementary teacher was challenged or a class rule was broken, and how you reacted.*
   What to Say:
   - Relate a personal experience dealing with a class rule that is often broken. Explain a situation when students are not listening and carrying on a side conversation.
   - Have a class meeting and develop a rubric for accountable talk: "Listen to the Speaker. Raise your hand when you want to speak."
   - Self-reflect in the moment on how students are learning and systems for preventing problems. *Am I engaging the student in learning? Have I been clear in my expectations? Does the student understand the routines?*
   - Maintain student dignity. Don't make a big deal in front of the classroom. Increase proximity to student. If the behavior continues, focus on students' personal responsibility for off-task behavior. *What should you be doing right now? What rule should you be following?*
   - Relate to your system of providing consequences for on- and off-task behaviors.
   - Other considerations: Don't share personal experiences about the worst situation you've ever handled.

What Not to Say:
- My authority has never been challenged.
- I freaked out and didn't know what to do.

3. *What do you do when your elementary students are engaging in a lively small group, hands on activity or discussion and you want the whole class to listen to you?*
   What to Say:
   - Use an established routine ("the quiet signal") for smooth transitions from small group discussion to whole class.

- Move around the room and make positive statements about students who are on-task and ready to learn.
- To create smoother transitions, move around the room to each small group and quietly alert them, "Your group has two minutes to complete the discussion."

What Not to Say:
- Flick the lights on and off (response too brief).
- Shout across the room, "Is everybody ready?"'

Communication with Families

How would you communicate with parents that their child should be tested for special education services?
What to Say:
- Explain that you follow the established school protocol for recommending a student for test. Share all the interventions and processes that you have done prior to this point - be specific and share data!
- Talk with the parent about how the team believes that assessment would be critical to identify needs for learning and behavior. It should not come as a surprise to the parents if the teacher has been communicating effectively up to this point.
- Share information with tact and dignity.
- Talk about how testing is in the best interest of their child.

What Not to Say:
- Your child needs medicine.
- Your child is lazy.
- I think your child has a disability but the IEP team does not.
- We always test kids to move them to special programs to get the help they need.

Professionalism

How have you stayed current in your subject matter and in the field of teaching?
What to Say:
- I hold memberships in professional organizations related to my content area (s) (e.g. National Council of Teachers of Mathematics, International Reading Association)
- I read professional journals and books (name them) and attend conferences and workshops. Describe the last conference you attended and what you learned.
- I am enrolled in graduate courses that relate to my professional learning goals (to increase subject matter knowledge and/or pedagogy).
- Other considerations: If you're a recent graduate, discuss your professional learning plan in your hiring portfolio. State one of your goals and an action you have planned for the

future. Explain that you're interested in the district's professional development for helping teachers raise student achievement and mentoring programs for new teachers.

What Not to Say:
- I recently graduated so I am current. I've learned everything that I need to know at this point.
- I read the Internet and use Wikipedia extensively.

Common Interview Mistakes

Avoid standing out for the wrong reasons! Knowing what <u>not</u> to do during an interview is just as important as knowing what to do. CareerBuilders.com conducts an annual survey of nearly 2,500 hiring managers about common and unusual mistakes made by job applicants in interviews. Here are eight, most common mistakes made by job applicants with percent of hiring managers reporting the mistake.

- *Answer a cell phone or text during the interview* (71% reporting)
  <u>What to Do</u>: Turn off your cell phone before you enter the interview!

- *Dress inappropriately* (69% reporting)
  <u>What to Do</u>: Dress using professional attire.

- *Appear disinterested* (69% reporting)
  <u>What to Do</u>: Appear excited, enthusiastic, and committed. Smile when you walk into the interview. Smile periodically when responding to questions. When an interviewer poses a question, respond by saying "I'm glad you asked me that question. I've given the question careful consideration." Vary your tone of voice and rate of speaking. Sit up straight and provide eye contact to your interviewers.

- *Appear arrogant* (66% reporting)
  <u>What to Do</u>: Appear confident, not self-important. Use "I statements" and avoid making absolute statements. For instance, instead of saying "You should never use tangible rewards for completing homework." say "I've learned from personal experience that tangible rewards for positive behaviors have benefits and limitations."

- *Speak negatively about a current or previous employer* (63% reporting)
  <u>What to Do</u>: Speak positively about your prior experiences. Do not use the first and last names of people when explaining a personal experience. Remove students' real names on samples of student work in a hiring portfolio.

- *Chew gum* (59% reporting)
  <u>What to Do</u>: Arrive early, visit the restroom, and deposit your gum in the trash can!

- *Do not provide specific answers* (35% reporting)
  <u>What to Do</u>: Provide specific examples using your personal experience. "Here are three approaches I have used successfully: First, Second, Third.

- *Do not ask good questions* (32% reporting)
  <u>What to Do</u>: Before the interview, research the school and district. At the end of the interview ask the interviewers questions that convey understanding of the district. For example, ask "I understand from reading the student demographics on the district web site that 6-7% of your students are bilingual or ESL. How are these two programs for English language learners working? Which strategies are most effective for raising student achievement?"

Your Professional Image
Here is advice to improve your professional image.

<u>Personal Health</u>
Be rested, healthy, vibrant, and clean. Groom well. Smell good and sweeten your breath with mouthwash or a powerful mint. Remove gum before you enter the building.

<u>Arrive Early and Turn Off Your Cell Phone</u>
Interviewers highly value job applicants who arrive 5-10 minutes early. Study the directions to the school building to avoid taking wrong turns and being late. Arrive 30 minutes before the scheduled interview. Wait in the car or a nearby coffee shop until it's time. Turn off your cell phone before you enter the building.

<u>The Greeting</u>
Typically, a job applicant enters a room with 5-10 interview committee members who are seated. Upon entering, it is customary for a job applicant to introduce him/herself and greet each interviewer with eye contact, smile and a firm handshake. Gripping the fingertips may be considered feminine, but is not considered appropriate in this situation. Be prepared to make some small talk before you begin.

<u>Eye Contact</u>
Interviewers will notice if you do not make eye contact with them while speaking. If you look away from someone who is speaking with you, they may interpret this as low confidence. You aren't staring at them, but rather, you're looking comfortably. After the interviewer delivers the question, shift your eye contact to other members of the committee. Draw them in by providing eye contact.

<u>Facial Expressions and Posture</u>
Ask someone you trust to assess what your facial expressions and posture conveys. Practice

sitting at your kitchen table as if you are in the room for the interview. Think about where you will place your hands. Place your hands on the table next to your portfolio. Occasionally use your hands for expression. Communicate in an open, engaged, friendly, and alert manner. Smile often and use appropriate eye contact. Do not slouch. Convey greater confidence by sitting up or standing straight.

Dress for Success
Dressing well is respectful - a compliment to your interviewers. You want to dress appropriately but not make your attire a distraction. Dress conservatively. Everything should be clean and pressed. Men and women should wear matched two-piece suits. The color can be navy, dark gray, or black. The fabric can be wool, wool blend, or good quality microfiber. During the summer, wear more comfortable fabrics.

Men should wear an attractive, coordinated silk tie and long-sleeved white or light blue solid or conservative striped shirt, polished leather dress shoes, and dark socks. Avoid character ties. Remove earrings. Cologne should be used sparingly or not at all.

Women should wear a two-piece matched pant or dress suit and closed-toe shoes. Skirt lengths should be at the knee or lower. Underneath the suit jacket, wear a tailored, collared blouse in a color or small print that coordinates with your suit. Don't show cleavage. Be conservative with make-up and jewelry. Perfume should be used sparingly or not at all.

Bring a small briefcase or business-like tote bag containing your hiring portfolio, a folder with cover letters clipped to résumés, a notepad and pen, and cell phone.

Thank You Letters
About two days after you meet with the interviewing committee, compose an electronic business-style letter for each interviewer. Timeliness is important. As we move into the 21st Century, the etiquette for formal communication with prospective employers is changing. It's acceptable to deliver an electronic letter as an attached file. Transmit the letter as an attached PDF file.

Before attaching the e-letter to an email, develop the letter in a word-processing program. Insert an electronic signature image after the closing. Proofread the letter carefully and then save the document as a PDF. Then attach the file. The text in the actual email message area should be short and professional.

Example of a Thank You Letter to Interviewers

Albert Einstein
60 Genius Blvd., Princeton, NJ 08542
(609) 345-6789
aeinstein@njc.edu

June 17, 2010

Ms. Maria Santos, Director
Department of Human Resources
Providence Public Schools
97 Westminster Street
Providence, NJ 08765

Dear Ms. Santos,

Thank you so much for the opportunity to interview for the elementary classroom teaching position in Providence Public Schools.

Here is additional evidence of my competence as a teacher, please copy this URL into your web browser and view my hiring portfolio. The components are aligned to the Providence Public Schools' five domains of effective teaching (selection criteria) and five teacher competencies.

URL: http://www.aeinsteinhiringportfolio.com

I was delighted to hear about the recent funding for the PASA afterschool inquiry science and math programs. This will be a great way to motivate under-represented groups to pursue math-science through middle and high school. I look forward to having a role in this important program. I have the leadership skills needed to coordinate the program.

I'm fully committed to working with Providence to help all learners achieve high standards! I look forward to hearing your decision and excited about starting my teaching career in Providence.

Sincerely,

Albert Einstein

Albert Einstein

Post Online Applications

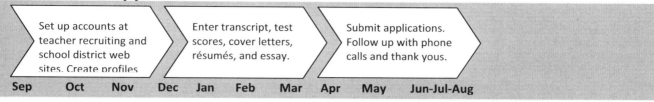

Set up accounts at teacher recruiting and school district web sites. Create profiles	Enter transcript, test scores, cover letters, résumés, and essay.	Submit applications. Follow up with phone calls and thank yous.

Sep   Oct   Nov   Dec   Jan   Feb   Mar   Apr   May   Jun-Jul-Aug

Increasingly, schools and districts are posting job openings at teacher recruitment web sites and receiving applications filed electronically by job applicants. For employers, online recruitment reduces the cost and time of advertising in newspapers and the paperwork of managing the hiring process. Hiring committees can easily review, share and screen online application materials. There is no need for photocopying and mailing materials.

For the job applicant, you can save time and money and stay organized by setting up a profile and centralizing your job application materials. There is no cost for photocopying and mailing applications. Some sites charge the job applicant a monthly fee to use the recruitment services. Other sites charge the employers a fee and it's free to the job applicant. However, they may charge for additional services such as official verification of transcripts, data entry of job application materials, or transmitting application packages to any employer outside the teacher recruitment site.

Teacher Recruitment and Hiring Web Sites

ABCTeachingJobs.com
EducationCrossing.com
EdZapp.com
SchoolSpring.com
TeacherJobs.com
Teachers.net
Teachers-Teachers.com

Online Job Search, Application and Hiring Process

The process varies at different sites. Typically, job-seekers begin the process by creating a job applicant account and receiving login information (e.g., username and password).

Next, the applicant develops a universal application. Standard items include a cover letter and résumé. Complete these documents offline using a word processing application and proofreading. Copy and paste the text from these documents into your application. Customize these items for different positions and modify them at any time.

Add other items such as transcripts, standardized test scores, licenses and certifications, letters of recommendations, and responses to essay questions. Some services provide a site for organizing and posting a showcase teaching portfolio that includes evidence of your knowledge and skill of teaching, samples of student work, a philosophy statement, and digital images.

Users connect to schools and districts in several ways. You can set up job preferences and receive email alerts or search for job postings based on your job preferences. Or, you can post your profile so recruiters can invite you to apply for position.

When you're ready to apply for a job, simply click "Submit." You can track multiple job applications simultaneously and receive emails from employers when your application has been received and invited for interviews.

If you make a mistake after submitting, you can withdraw your application and re-submit.

Other Job Posting Sites

In addition to teacher recruitment and hiring websites listed previously, consider the following job-posting sites for different public, charter, religious education, and independent schools.

- Local newspaper classifieds
- College and University Career Centers
- State Department of Education – Department of Human Resources
- US Regional Education Applicant Placement (REAP) System
- Independent Schools: Carney, Sandoe and Associates and National Association of Independent Schools

Teaching Abroad

If you're adventurous, consider applying for teaching jobs in international schools or teaching English as a foreign language. It's a great way to make a difference in another part of the world and bring the benefits of the experiences back home.

U.S. Department of State partners with independent non-governmental schools to serve children of Department of State civilian employees. American-sponsored schools overseas contract with private organizations in recruiting teachers. For example, the International School Services recruits for approximately 200 international American schools worldwide, including community-sponsored, company-sponsored, and proprietary institutions. In most cases, the curriculum is U.S.-oriented and English is the language of instruction. Contracts are for two years.

United States Department of Defense schools serve the children of military service members and Department of Defense civilian employees throughout the world. The Department of Defense operates nearly 200 public schools in 14 districts located in 12 foreign countries, seven states, Guam, and Puerto Rico.

English language teaching opportunities exist throughout the world. Opportunities for teaching depend on where you want to teach, what level you want to teach, and your background and qualifications. You do not need to speak the host country's language; however, it is beneficial. TESOL Teachers of Speakers of Other Languages provides information such as general qualifications for teachers planning to teach English to speakers of other languages and an online Career Center for job listings.

You can teach as a Peace Corps education volunteer in Africa, Asia, the Caribbean, Central and South America, Europe, and the Middle East. Education volunteers promote world peace and friendship and teach in a community overseas for 27 months. They introduce innovative teaching methods and integrate health education and environmental awareness into different subject areas. The application process takes 6-12 months.

References

American Association of Employment in Education. (2011). *2011 AAEE job search handbook.* Columbus,

Bureau of Labor/Statistics Department of Labor, Occupational Outlook Handbook, 2010-2011 Edition. Retrieved from http://www.bls.gov/oco/ocos069.htm

Clement, Mary. (2006, Spring). The game has changed: Tips for finding a new teaching position. *Kappa Delta Pi Record.* 155-119.

Clement, Mary. (2008, January/February). Improving teacher selection with behavior-based interviewing. *Principal.* 44-47.

Daly, Tim & Kramer, Matt Kramer. (2007, July). *Improving teacher selection to improve student results at* National Association of System Heads Tenth Annual State Teams PK-16 Institute Minneapolis, July 29-31, 2007. New Teacher Project /Teacher for America.

Kniseley, Greg, Vesey, Melissa, and Zakin, Rebecca. (2009). Winning a teaching position in a tight job market. *2011 AAEE Job Search Handbook.* American Association of Employment in Education. pp. 4-6.

Kniseley, Greg. (2009). *Elementary principal survey on market conditions and hiring factors.* Providence, RI: Rhode Island College.

Providence School Department. Criterion-based hiring and staffing assignment process. Retrieved July 21, 2009 from http://www.providenceschools.org

Theel, Ronald and Tallerico, Marilyn. (2004, Spring). Using portfolios for teacher hiring: Insights from school principals. *Action in Teacher Education,* 26 (1) 26-33.

US Department of Education, Office of Postsecondary Education. "Teacher Shortage Areas by State." Retrieved from http://www2.ed.gov/about/offices/list/ope/pol/tsa.html

Wasicsko, M. M. (2006). Determining dispositions to teach: A hiring strategy. *Principal* 86 (1) 51-52.

Wasicsko, M. M. (2004). The 20-minute hiring assessment. *School Administrator.* 61 (9) 40-42.

Career Center Directors

Bring *Winning a Teaching Position in Any Job Market* ™ course, presentation, or workshop to your campus!

What students say about Professor Kniseley's course:

"One of the most effective workshops of any kind that I have ever participated in."

"Presentations, materials, and guidance were first-rate . . . a tremendous bargain for the cost."

"CURR 480 has provided me with excellent preparation for the job application process. I am glad I took this class before student teaching."

Contact Professor Kniseley who can present an interactive workshop and consult with you to customize a course for your education students and alumni.

MacGregor Kniseley, Ed. D.
HM 209, Department of Elementary Education
Rhode Island College Providence, RI 02908
p - (401) 456-8865   e – mkniseley2@gmail.com
Website - http://www.winateachingjob.com

9855344R0005

Made in the USA
Charleston, SC
19 October 2011